# Robert Graves and the White Goddess

Edited by John B. Vickery

Myth and Literature: Contemporary Theory and Practice (1966)

# Robert Graves and the White Goddess

## JOHN B. VICKERY

UNIVERSITY OF NEBRASKA PRESS • LINCOLN

INTERNATIONAL STANDARD BOOK NUMBER 0-8032-0817-0

LIBRARY OF CONGRESS CATALOG CARD NUMBER 70-183363

MANUFACTURED IN THE UNITED STATES OF AMERICA

FOR MY DAUGHTER

# Contents

# Preface

This book is a study of Robert Graves's mythopoeic thought, its genesis, nature, and contours. Since it does not pretend to be a complete treatment of his poetry, fiction, or criticism, I have not found it appropriate to deal, either in the text or the notes, with the views or interpretations of other critics. Myth is so central to Graves's work that a firm understanding of its forms and functions allows the interested reader a crucial mode of access to his literary canon in general and to his poetry in particular. If we understand what his myth consists of and how it is deployed, we are placed in a fair way to grasping the main features of his thought and art.

Of all the elements in Graves's work the most far-reaching and important is clearly that of the White Goddess, who, in his view, is the multifaceted great fertility goddess of the original matriarchal age in all civilizations. In that period women, as her representatives, were the politically and socially dominant power, but for a variety of reasons—intellectual, emotional, and political —this order was overturned just when prehistory and myth emerged into history. The goddess of passion and fertility was replaced by a god of reason who directed mankind's attention away from the world of nature and its ritual of the seasons. From this dislocation, Graves argues, follow virtually all the ills to which contemporary mankind is heir. For him the chief of these is the poet's separation from the goddess, his true Muse, and his loss of the original and essential language of poetry, namely, myth, which was based on a close knowledge of the seasons and vegetative life. Recovering this language allows the poet to render his quintessential theme—the birth, life, death, and resurrection of the dying and reviving god whom the poet associates with himself. In the course of his life the god struggles first to win and then to retain the love of the White Goddess, who has the threefold form of mother, wife or lover, and layer-out. With his ultimate loss both of her love and his life he faces the final test of his understanding of the true poetic theme, life and death mediated by love.

In postulating the divine figure of the White Goddess, Graves moves beyond his sources concerning ancient fertility goddesses to discover a single female form who embraces a range of roles, from orgiastic tyrant to serene helpmate. Essentially, she is a conceptual myth founded on ritual and functional similarities in deities whose worship is historically verified. No one except Graves ever worshipped her, though many peoples may have worshipped goddesses one of whose attributes was whiteness. She is a creature of almost infinitely metamorphic nature who changes her guises, roles, and qualities as well as her name. These changes are correlated to various natural and human phases so that she is both a radically chameleonic figure through-out the entirety of human life and also a single, enduring, archetypal creature. The more one reads Graves, however, the more it becomes clear that the White Goddess is not simply an entity feared and revered in dimmest antiquity, but also repre-sents the entire chameleonlike relationship obtaining between man and his environment. In a very real sense, she is both the natural and psychological worlds in which man must live subject to forces other than his own untrammeled will. As such, she is a creature charged equally with infinite attractiveness and danger. Her objectification in the lineaments of a beautiful yet cruel woman is an imaginative emblem. Actually the White Goddess is an extended metaphor for the vicissitudes and exaltation that come to man from the external world of nature and society and from the internal world of his own metabolism and psyche.

With these concepts in mind it is possible to see how Graves utilizes the White Goddess to structure his work and lend it significance. His most characteristic poems are tautly controlled renderings of a single facet of the relations between man and man. Yet because of the White Goddess's multiple nature even the most commonplace events and moods share the mythic pattern of attraction, struggle, and defeat, of birth, life, and death. Similarly, Graves's view of her nature explains the recurring presence of the compound of courage, honesty, and regard that dominates his poetry. Breaking the cycle of birth-death-rebirth is the grossest violation of the goddess's ritual and of the pattern of existence she represents, which, Graves would argue, is the only imaginative possibility available to man. Because the goddess is simultaneously woman, nature, and one's own unconscious, to deny her is to break with ritual. By refusing to desire and love her, by evading her loss, one exposes himself to the unmediated and incomprehensible terrors of desolation, perversion, and destruction.

The White Goddess can be flouted only at the individual's peril because her ritual embodies the fundamental and ineluctable course of life itself. To avoid her in order to remain safe, retain tranquility, and stay alive is to be guilty of presumptuous self-sufficiency. To treasure life passionately and to struggle, however vainly, against its termination best shows the goddess the exalted value one places on her initial gift of life. Thus, to be a victim of the goddess is no mere personal indulgence in the possible disasters of romantic love. Rather it is a solemn duty arising out of man's inevitable commitment to desire and endeavor, to wish and action, and its termination by his mortality. By accepting the rhythm of nature and celebrating its fructification and flowering in the human expression of life, the individual learns not simply his or her subjection to mortality but more importantly the value, beauty, and pleasure of the human season of fertility. It is in this light that Graves views the role of the poet as central to the imaginative life of man. The true poet knows the ecstasy, the hardships, and the eventual annihilation stemming from the struggle with poetic language and yet eagerly accepts the destruction of his own self in order that a new and better creature —an eternal being, a poem—may be born.

In this study my starting point is Graves's reliance in *The White Goddess* on Sir James Frazer's *The Golden Bough*. The connections between Frazer and Graves are both subtle and extensive. Although obviously Frazer is far from the only influence on the poet's vision, he is a major shaping factor both in *The White Goddess* and the poetry which makes up Graves's most sustained claim to our attention. Moreover, *The Golden Bough* lies behind the bulk of current literary interest in the subject of myth and ritual. Because Frazer is the major informing presence and tutelary genius for the modern mythopoeic imagination, it is particularly important to determine as accurately as possible when Graves initially came under his sway. Chapter 1 attends both to this question and to the nature of Graves's first poetic use of myth and Frazer-inspired attitudes. It shows how many of the later convictions and themes existed in embryonic and frequently tentative fashion from the outset.

Chapter 2 turns to the dominant mythic motifs and their interrelations as developed in *The White Goddess* and *King Jesus*. The former is shown to be a displacement (in Northrop Frye's sense of the term) and complication of the central topics of *The Golden Bough*. The latter is demonstrated to be the clearest fictive rendering by Graves of *The White Goddess*'s stress on the importance of submission to the goddess and her rituals. It develops the signal importance of the figures of the scapegoat and the fertility goddess as well as the intricate dynamics and rituals of both figures as these are worked out in the lives of human beings. Such themes also encourage that ironic, quizzical compounding of tenderness and tough-mindedness which becomes the dominant attitude in the mature lyrics.

In the remaining chapters the emphasis falls almost exclusively on Graves's poetry, focusing upon the poetry as a coherent mythopoeic rendering of man's roles and relationships in three distinct but interwoven worlds. Chapter 3 deals with poems of what I call the human world. They constitute, it is argued, devotional rites given over to recognizing the divine, preternatural character of life. Here the multiplicity of roles under which the goddess and her human victim appear is charted in detail as are Graves's rendering of phallic myths and classical legends for the same celebratory purpose. Man, however, subsists for Graves midway between natural and unnatural worlds; and Chapter 4 examines those poems which treat of the natural world as fact and as emblem. Out of the fact of nature three central motifs are developed: the rhythms of fertility and sterility, the cyclical pattern of time and experience, and nature's intermittent assumption of human and divine forms, which leads directly to the emblematic function of nature. This is seen to be compounded of fertility rituals, to involve the matching of desire and reality, and to be equivalent to the goddess herself. As a result, many of these poems are educative in character, apprising man both of nature's dangers and her benefits and of the relation between her and myth and deity.

Finally, Chapter 5 explores poems of the unnatural, the other world, poems which attend to spirits, nightmares, ghosts, spells, and the like. Ultimately these are seen as the prime antagonist to man's comprehension of nature and as impingement on the human world variously as threat, trial or test, and as punishment. The conclusion explains the importance of the poet and language in Graves's eyes. For him, man best exists in the three worlds by being a poet, that is, a disciplined, dedicated user of language. It is the poet who keeps the balance between language employed as the deflector of raw, brute experience and as a means of retreating from reality. Poetic language is man's way of acknowledging both the natural and the other worlds without being absorbed into them. Here the importance of Graves's satires emerge clearly, for they mediate scrupulously between the personal lyrics of love and the more nearly epical cast of the sequence explicitly concerned with the White Goddess. The satires on classical legends best serve this function, for their role, and that of the satires generally, is to prevent the dissolution of awe and mystery upon which both the worship of the White Goddess and the apprehension of the nature of human life stand.

# Robert Graves and the White Goddess

# CHAPTER I

# The Origins of the Myth

When Robert Graves published *The White Goddess* in 1948, he exhibited the impact of *The Golden Bough* in unmistakable terms. In theme, detail, method, and authority *The White Goddess* invokes Frazer's work repeatedly. Since then the central thesis and concern of that book has come to dominate much of his poetry as well as his criticism. As a result he may be viewed as the living writer most deeply affected not only by *The Golden Bough* but by the whole corpus of Frazer's writing. Unlike Eliot, he draws from Frazer not merely a tone or attitude and specific insights but a general pattern concerning the nature of poetry, its relation to religion and society, and the education of the poet. And unlike Lawrence, he reflects *The Golden Bough* less by a process of casual absorption and empathy than by an exhaustively detailed study of the text itself.

If his knowledge of Frazer is as intimate as appears from *The White Goddess*, *The Nazarene Gospel Restored*, and his edition of *The Greek Myths*, when was it acquired? At first glance one would suggest the 1930s as a probable point of origin, for it was then that he first started writing novels with a classical and therefore incipiently comparative religion background. His mining of classical sources for his novels undoubtedly contributed to his interest in myth and ritual. Yet a closer look at his earlier writing reveals both a familiarity with and predisposition toward the language and problems of myth.

Though Graves had issued five small volumes of poetry before his first book of criticism appeared, the surest evidence for his knowledge of myth and *The Golden Bough* in particular can be found in his early critical works. On *English Poetry* (1922), his first published prose work, contains his first explicit reference to Frazer. In interpreting Keats's "La Belle Dame Sans Merci" as the author's covert identification of "the woman he loved and the death he feared," [1] Graves suggests that Keats, like *The Golden Bough*, is speaking to those who can endure having their most valued experiences analyzed without ceasing to value them. [2] This obviously does not demonstrate anything more than Graves's general familiarity with the attitudes and effects of Frazer's work. A comment some six years later, however, reveals both a general sense of Frazer's impact on contemporary poetry and a knowledge of specific details derived from *The Golden Bough*. In *A Survey of Modernist Poetry* (1928), written in conjunction with Laura Riding, he points out that many writers "have borrowed extensively from Sir James Frazer's comparative study of primitive myths" [3] and cites as an instance Sacheverell Sitwell's allusion to the ritual slaying of fair-haired men as representatives of the corn god. [4] Apparently, even apart from any other evidence, by 1928 Graves was sufficiently interested in Frazer to be able to detect highly specific allusions to aspects of his work.

There is additional evidence to suggest that Graves was aware of and responsive to many of the general implications of *The Golden Bough* before 1928. For instance, in On *English Poetry* he links poetry to magic and the poet to the witch doctor, echoing Frazer's contention that religion was descended from magic. [5] Again referring to *The Golden Bough* in the same essay, he emphasizes primitive man's interest in dreams and suggests that the verbal restrictions of taboo, so exhaustively discussed by Frazer, contributed markedly to the development of poetry's dream symbolism. [6] Further support for Graves's familiarity with

1. Robert Graves, *On English Poetry* (London: Heinemann, 1922), p. 51.
2. Ibid., pp. 54-55.
3. Graves and Riding, *A Survey of Modernist Poetry* (London: Heinemann, 1928), p. 171.
4. Ibid., p. 172.
5. *On English Poetry*, p. 19.
6. Ibid., pp. 19-20.

Frazer by at least 1922 is found in *Poetic Unreason* (1925), whose initial chapter was an address given in December, 1922. In this chapter he asserts that nursery rhymes and fables are the residue of ancient history and thought, a view that reflects Frazer's contention that folk beliefs and customs are the remnants of their primitive versions.[7]

And in the course of arguing for the relativity of values in poetry, he adduces as illustrations two strikingly anthropological references. One is the custom of primitive religions' converting the god of their most powerful enemy into their devil. This is paralleled, says Graves, by Christians before the Reformation regarding Faunus as a devil.[8] In this he is reiterating one of Frazer's most frequently made points, that Christianity develops through incorporating pagan primitive myths, rituals, and deities, and that religion generally maintains its primacy through internecine strife. The other anthropological point, tested by experiment with an Indian friend, is that literary and cultural symbols are both astonishingly common to diverse cultures and at the same time not universal or common to all cultures.[9] The comparativist emphasis shared with Frazer is stressed by Graves's observation that "even such simple symbols as we have in common with the Hindus are unintelligible to Congo pigmy and Eskimo."[10] Similarly, when he points out that the Bible and Christianity are not the only sources nor unique repositories of conventional symbolism, he clearly implies, with Frazer, both the relevance of other religions and sacred books and their continuity with Christianity as matrices of symbol formation.

In the remainder of the book, which may have been written later than 1922, Graves continues to demonstrate his familiarity with the anthropological world of *The Golden Bough*. Thus, he rejects the view of Burns's poem "John Barleycorn" as "a simple allegory" of the transformation of barley into whiskey and argues

---

7. Graves, *Poetic Unreason* (London: Cecil Palmer, 1925), p. 33.
8. Ibid., p. 43.
9. Ibid., pp. 35-36.
10. Ibid., p. 36.

that its "allusions are appropriate to the story of the life, death, and resurrection of Jesus Christ." [11] To buttress this view, he cites *The Divine Mystery* of Allen Upward, who with the aid of *The Golden Bough* interprets the poem as dealing with ancient Pictish rituals of human sacrifice. He disagrees with Upward's reading largely because at this time he is more concerned with advancing his "conflict" theory of poetic genesis and meaning. Nevertheless, he does suggest that Burns's source was probably "the last form, the nursery-game form, of an ancient tradition of blood sacrifice." [12] Whether Graves was drawn to a consideration of Burns's poem by Frazer's reference to it in his *Adonis, Attis, Osiris* volume is, of course, impossible to tell. Certainly he was aware of this dimension of the poem and *The Golden Bough* figured significantly in shaping that awareness.

Further evidence of his familiarity with developments in anthropology and comparative religion at the end of the nineteenth century appears in his casual reference to the solar myth controversy inspired by Max Müller and in his specific declaration of familiarity with Jane Harrison's *Ancient Art and Ritual*.[13] Similarly, in concluding his discussion of George Herbert's "The Bag," he observes that the divine figure is fused with that of the temptress and adds that "primitive art, particularly sacred art, is full of these double figures." [14] These assertions seem likely to have derived their easy assurance from Frazer's discussion of Artemis, Astarte, and Demeter and Persephone. The initial volumes of *The Golden Bough*, namely, *The Magic Art and the Evolution of Kings*, lie behind Graves's reiterated stress not only upon the affinities of poetry and magic but on the historical existence of a belief in witchcraft and wizardry.[15] Their stamp is also visible in his association of the emotional, the associative, and the primitive as a mode of thought.[16]

11. Ibid., pp. 63, 64.
12. Ibid., p. 68.
13. Ibid., pp. 66, 275, respectively.
14. Ibid., pp. 62-63.
15. *On English poetry*, pp. 19-20; *Poetic Unreason*, pp. 158-59, 166.
16. *Poetic Unreason*, pp. 55, 126.

A concluding instance of perhaps a more specific character appears in the chapter on "Poetic Genius," a concept which he says has been "most intelligible hitherto in the context of mankind's struggle for the divine." [17] Here, he semifacetiously suggests that the British king and royal family are divine and hence segregated and totemized.[18] He also applies Frazer's idea about the intimate interrelation of king, deity, and subjects to the feudal system with an irony reminiscent of Frazer's own account of humanity's "search for the god-man." [19] Thus, he argues that Jehovah, Athena, and John Bull are all the spirits of their subjects regarded as tribal gods. Such a notion is implicit in *The Golden Bough*, but because of Frazer's rationalistic psychology and his antipathy to Freudian and other psychologies of the unconscious, it was left to Jane Harrison, who had absorbed the theories of Durkheim and the French sociological school, to develop for English scholars a concept of the god as a psychological projection of a group feeling. Consequently, it would appear possible that Graves was acquainted by this time with her *Prolegomena* and *Themis* as well as Frazer's *Golden Bough*, which would indicate that problems of myth and religion were of more than casual interest to him even this early in his career.

## II

The evidence so far presented is essentially part of intellectual history and the tides of taste. The really central question for the present study, however, is the kind of impact *The Golden Bough* has had on the poetry and fiction of Robert Graves. While this external evidence is important, it serves mainly as a series of clues bearing on Graves's only other early writing, his poetry. Essentially, we are concerned with two questions here. First, do any of the poems which antedate Graves's first prose work (*On English Poetry*, 1922) [20] show a familiarity with *The Golden*

---

17. Ibid., p. 242.
18. Ibid.
19. Ibid.
20. The bibliography in *Collected Poems, 1914-1926* (London: Heinemann, 1927) lists the date as 1921, but this appears to be a misprint. Cf. Douglas Day, *Swifter Than Reason* (Chapel Hill: University of North Carolina Press, 1963), p. 218.

*Bough?* And secondly, what is the nature of Graves's use of Frazer when he does become acquainted with him? Connecting these two questions is a third, what was the character of Graves's other interests which might have predisposed him to respond vigorously to Frazer when he did make his acquaintance?

Of the poems in his first collection, *Over the Brazier,* none show unmistakable signs of Frazer's influence. This is not remarkable since eleven of the poems were written while he was a schoolboy at Charterhouse. Furthermore, the collection as a whole appeared when Graves was only twenty-one, by which time he had been in the army for two years and so presumably had little time for reading, especially lengthy anthropological classics.[21] Nevertheless, one of these poems does stand out as suggestive of Graves's later religious interests and mythopoeic techniques. "In the Wilderness" deals with Christ's forty-day trial in the wilderness, but the poet has added the annual scape-goat of the Old Testament as his companion. Critics have described it as sentimental and romantic while even Graves affects to be contemptuous of it.[22] Yet despite a chequered career of inclusion and omission from sundry volumes, it opens the *Collected Poems* (1959); in the foreword to this collection Graves suggests that only those poems which pass muster with the author are included.

Clearly its retention is not merely designed to represent the poet's juvenilia. It is kept despite not really being a good poem because it has a thematic or symbolic role of some significance. For the author of *King Jesus* to have thirty years before linked Christ and the scapegoat as complementary images is warrant

---

21. In *Good-bye to All That* (London: J. Cape, 1929), p. 213, Graves remarks that the only books he had in France were copies of Keats and Blake. At the same time (p. 231), he records that it was commonplace in the instructors' mess to describe God and Gott "as opposed tribal deities." Such a descriptive phrase, if indeed not simply an afterthought, argues for a minimal anthropological awareness and one that may have contributed to the trench soldier's lack of "religious feeling of even the crudest kind" (p. 230). Corroboration of this last is provided by other poets such as Wilfred Owens in "At a Calvary near the Amre" and "Le Christianisme."

22. Day, *Swifter Than Reason,* p. 6; J. M. Cohen, *Robert Graves* (New York: Grove Press, 1961), p. 11; *Good-bye to All That,* p. 21.

enough for feeling that whether aided by comparative religionists or not, Graves had already, perhaps intuitively, recognized the dominant role Christ was to play in his imagination, that of the sacred king-scapegoat. And by having an actual goat as Christ's comrade in the wilderness, Graves points up both the biblical source and the primitive nature of the concept. At the same time, the phrase "the guileless young scapegoat" effectively links goat and Christ as sin-bearers, thereby marking the expansion of the concept to include, as Frazer chronicled in Volume 9 of *The Golden Bough*, human beings as well as animals and inanimate objects.[23]

Whether Frazer can be added to Holman Hunt as an inspiration for the poem is uncertain. Nevertheless, it is a fact that Graves's view of Christ as the perfect man is remarkably close to that of *The Golden Bough*. Both stress the human rather than the supernatural qualities. Another adumbrative feature of the poem is its quasi-emblematic use of bird and animal imagery. The she-pelican, basilisk, and cockatrice are all employed because of traditional associations which intensify the stress upon Christ's power to command their attention. Such images anticipate Graves's later works in which natural phenomena like animals, birds, and trees have highly specific symbolic import much of which is codified for us in *The White Goddess*. And as we shall see later, a great deal of the symbolism as well as the controlling idea derives from *The Golden Bough*.

"In the Wilderness" hints at Graves's later interest in Christian and Hebrew myth and legend. A similar function is fulfilled by several poems in his second volume, *Fairies and Fusiliers*. In "To Robert Nichols," a war poet and author of "Faun's Holiday," Graves rejects the idea of writing about life renewed as a young and goatlike creature because it is the season of winter and death when "ice grips at branch and root, / And singing birds are mute." The diction describing Nichols's Pan is conventional ("gay

---

23. In the poem's original version *old* was used instead of *young*. The change seems to be dictated by Graves's desire to emphasize the parallel between Christ and goat through unity of tone and effect.

goatish brute," "red and rolling eye," "wanton lute," "lips dark with juicy stain"). On the other hand, Graves does concentrate on the qualities of intoxication, ecstasy, and sensuality which move through the fauns and Pan to culminate in Dionysus, whom Frazer described as not simply a god of the vine but of trees and agriculture generally. He superimposes life at the war front on a traditional Georgian scene of "vague music and green trees, / Hot sun and gentle breeze, / England in June attire." By this Graves can be seen groping tentatively for that juxtaposition of life and death, winter and summer, and their dramatic battles, which dominate so many of the pages of *The Golden Bough* and which, transmuted with subtle complexity, is at the very core of *The White Goddess*.

A somewhat similar theme is developed in "Faun" which dramatizes the creature's dispossession as a divine king. In so doing, its imagery suggests that the dispossession is the result of a shift in the modes of religious worship. This in turn has followed from the intrusion of a nameless "they" who have overrun and abused his sanctuary. Here, in a raw and elementary form, is Graves's thesis concerning myth's recording of politico-religious history, especially of tribal migrations.

What these poems do is testify to Graves's initial though undeveloped intimation that primitive religion is essentially a matter of fertility figures and rites and that the evolution of religion entails the curtailment and denial of this fact. Both of these points are Frazerian in character. What obscures this fact is the poetic tone, which is a compound of decorous Georgian pastoral and the neopaganism of Rupert Brooke. The conclusion is apparent. If Graves had not yet made himself familiar with *The Golden Bough*, he at least had started to formulate poetic ideas that would lead him to seize eagerly upon Frazer when the acquaintance was finally made. The same relationship obtains between *The Golden Bough* and such poems as "Babylon," "Letter to S.S. from Mametz Wood," and "Cherry-Time." The only difference is that of theme. These poems reveal Graves's early propensity to identify the world of magic, fairies, witches, and ghosts with that of the child and by extention the poet.

"Babylon," for instance, is essentially a neo-Romantic redaction of Wordsworth's Intimations Ode. Childhood is a time of spring and fairies and Babylon is a symbol of enchantment destroyed by wisdom, which is identified with "Truth and Reason." By growing up, the child ruthlessly scatters all the creatures of traditional fairy tales to the wilds of wood and cave leaving only "a few ghosts / Of timorous heart." There is, however, an important difference between Wordsworth and Graves: the latter laments not the loss of "celestial light" or "the visionary gleam" but the destruction of characters from folk and fairy tales. It is as if he agrees with R. R. Marett, an evolutionary anthropologist who shared many of Frazer's views, that "there is an underworld in which all have been reared, namely, the nursery. It may, thanks to a nurse of the old-fashioned type, have direct relations with the other underworld of peasant folk-lore, but in any case it has an analogous tradition of its own, and one as conservative as any known to man. Here old-time values retain their spell." [24] Whether consciously or not, Graves finds in Babylon and the nursery story a core of traditional values which have room for magic and imagination.

The poignant regret over the destruction of this world is tempered in the verse letter to Siegfried Sassoon by the anticipation of a postwar recuperative holiday in Wales which abounds in fairies and ghosts and "poetry most splendid." Here Graves, Sassoon, and Robert Nichols will see places associated with legendary characters such as Shawn Knarlbrand and the wizard Gwydion and creatures like the "Dog-cat" who was finally brought to bay "after a four years' chase / From Thessaly and the woods of Thrace." They will discover places

> where in old Roman days,
> Before Revivals changed our ways,
> The Virgin 'scaped the Devil's grab,

24. Marett, *Psychology and Folk-lore* (New York: Macmillan Co., 1920), p. 111. The essay from which this quotation is taken first appeared in 1918 and so is not adduced as a source of influence. Still, such opinions were current in folklorist circles and Graves's father was a collector of folklore as well as a poet.

Printing her foot on a stone slab
With five clear toe-marks.

The psychological curative powers of such scenes will then,
Graves concludes, issue in a great creative release of their poetic
powers. From these and poems like them it is clear Graves began
his career with a lively sense of the nursery as a deliberately
cultivated awareness of the poetic significance of the ancient
past.[25] Both of these notions were to be deepened and encouraged
by his contact with *The Golden Bough*.

Though Graves himself avers that he cannot remember exactly
when he first read Frazer, Jane Harrison, and the other Cambridge anthropologists, there is some striking evidence that it
may have been prior to *Fairies and Fusiliers*.[26] This evidence
occurs in the poems of this volume that use overt mythical and
anthropological references. One of these, "Dead Cow Farm,"
uses a parody of what is presumably the Egyptian creation myth
of Hathor, the cow goddess, to define the nature and future of
trench warfare. In doing so, Graves not only alludes ironically
to a goddess mentioned by Frazer, he also sardonically utilizes
Frazer's favorite technique of connecting pagan myths with
Christian beliefs:

An ancient saga tells us how
In the beginning the First Cow
(For nothing living yet had birth
But Elemental tow on earth)
Began to lick cold stones and mud:
Under her warm tongue flesh and blood
Blossomed, a miracle to believe:
And so was Adam born, and Eve.

At the close of the poem, he again reflects *The Golden Bough*

25. In *Good-bye to All That*, p. 39, he asserts that from age fourteen he stressed his Irish
ancestry, derived from his father, which presumably included Celtic myth, legend, and
folklore.
26. See Day, *Swifter Than Reason*, p. 156 n. 6.

by focusing on the death of the deity as a summation of the human condition or at least of the warrior's condition. A somewhat similar adaptation of myth that reveals among other things the author's traditional classical education is "Escape." It presents his coma following wounding and his presumed death as a trip to the classical underworld from which he escapes by feeding Cerberus morphia on "army biscuit smeared with ration jam." Here, too, the mythic material is treated with rollicking ironic gusto, as when Proserpine clears his head and sets him on the road back to the world while "after me roared and clattered angry hosts / Of demons, heroes, and policeman-ghosts."

Here in rude outline is Graves's later penchant for writing mythical satire in which exuberance and invention are defining traits.[27] Of equal interest for his subsequent development is his linking of the individual human being with mythic patterns, a habit that integrally connects his poetry of whatever date and *The White Goddess*.[28] The same is true of his handling of Cerberus, for while he makes the monster's actions accord with the classical myths of Hercules, Psyche, and Aeneas, he also departs from them. Thus he makes Cerberus's three heads those of "lion, and lynx, and sow" and the colors of its "monstrous hairy carcase, red and dun." Thirty years later the same heads are ascribed to Cerberus in *The White Goddess* and the colors are those of the Hounds of Hell of British and Celtic folklore.[29] This last suggests that already Graves is making motions toward the poetry of mythic syncreticism to which *The Golden Bough* was to contribute so materially.

Finally, two other poems in this early collection employ anthropological material rather than classical myth and in so doing increase the possibilities of Graves's having been acquainted by this time with *The Golden Bough*. The first of these, "Love

27. See Northrop Frye, "Graves, Gods and Scholars," *Hudson Review*, 9 (Summer, 1956): 301.

28. See the Preface to *Collected Poems 1938* (London: Cassell, 1938), and cf. Cohen, *Robert Graves*, p. 2.

29. Graves, *The White Goddess* (New York: Vintage Books, 1958), pp. 36, 455-56. The first, unreviewed edition appeared in 1948 which is why I say *thirty* rather than forty years.

and Black Magic," is a dramatic narrative about a maiden who has learnt magic from her wizard stepfather and is engaged to another sorcerer but wishes simply for a soldier-lover. What takes this out of the class of poems inspired by fairy tales and the like is the fact that as she sits waiting for the wizard to return from the woods, "she gazes up with a weary smile / At the rafter-hanging crocodile, / The slowly swinging crocodile." The references to transformation into toad or lizard may smack of *The Sorcerer's Apprentice* and carry the rhythmic accents of Edward Lear, but at the same time they seem to give a comic glance at *The Golden Bough*'s accounts of the crocodile's respectful preservation by primitive peoples and its totemic role in such societies.

An even more emphatic fusion of Lear and Frazer occurs in "The Bough of Nonsense," a deliberately and absurdly fanciful dialogue between Sassoon and Graves. On returning from the war, they come on a famous bough of an oak where a "nonsense" had a nest and then they make up a facetious poem or "nonsense hymn" to hang "in a deep grove" of banana trees to be worshipped by the followers of nonsense. The poem goes on to note that "whosoever worships in that place, / He disappears from sight and leaves no trace." Obviously such a *jeu d'esprit* will not withstand heavy-handedness. Yet such a collocation of images as oak bough, sacred grove, temple of worship, and disappearance of the lone worshipper is unlikely without the aid of *The Golden Bough* and its opening discussion of the sacred oak grove of Nemi and the ritual succession of its lone warrior-priest.[30]

If this is so, then one finds here a very early use of Frazer's material for purposes quite other than those of symbolic profundity and religious solemnity such as we find in T. S. Eliot and the later Edith Sitwell. Instead, such primitive customs,

---

30. For that matter even the banana trees may derive from *The Golden Bough* as much as from lighthearted fancy. See James G. Frazer, *The Golden Bough*, 12 vols. (London: Macmillan & Co., 1915), 3:276, 286, for their use as religious repositories. And in Frazer, *The Belief in Immortality*, 3 vols. (London: Macmillan & Co., 1913), 1:72-74, they figure as one of four main types of myth of the origin of death and are described as "a sad emblem of mortality" (p. 74).

striking the mind as bizarre and absurd, are utilized as elements from a real world which underscore the poetic mood of wild comedy verging on hysteria. In such a mood, to find life abounding in features as ridiculous as anyone can imagine is to intensify the original comedy. The transformation of this attitude toward primitive beliefs into one of more knowledgeable sympathy is one of the more striking aspects of Graves's poetic career. This may in part be due to a gradual deepening of his familiarity with and understanding of *The Golden Bough* and all those other works which either augment or derive from it.

A significant step in the direction of this transformation is found in several poems in *Whipperginny* published in 1923. Thus, "An Idyll of Old Age" retells the myth of Philemon and Baucis but in the ironic accents of Aldous Huxley's "Leda" which appeared at about the same time. It thereby continues the sardonic note of "Dead Cow Farm" though transposed to the cooler, more sophisticated tone of postwar life. Both poems reflect the skeptical temper of their time, shaped by such diverse elements as World War I, the "debunking" of Lytton Strachey's *Eminent Victorians*, and the publication of *The Golden Bough*. Similar in tone is "The Bowl and the Rim," which might be described as a semicomic dramatization of comparative religion as concentrated in Christian and Jewish reactions to Christ. The broad irony derives from two features: the reconciliation of an imprisoned rabbi and friar so that each assumes the other's basic religious criticism of Christ, and the refrain, which epitomizes the skeptic's view of Christ:

> Man-like he lived, but God-like died,
> All hatred from His thought removed,
> Imperfect until crucified,
> In crucifixion well-beloved.

Of a related order is "The Manifestation in the Temple," which is a Browningesque monologue in couplets about the speaker's rejection of such Hebrew priestly rites as sacrificing a white bull in favor of simple direct prayer "between my God and

me." Such antiritualism might have been one kind of response to
Frazer's lengthy and frequently ironic chronicling of the many
forms of ritual by which mankind has sought to coerce a supernatural world to his bidding. But it is another facet of the poem
which adumbrates the later Gravesian attitude to religious
phenomena. Confronted with a scene in which "the tall gilt
image of God at the altar niche / Wavers and stirs," then speaks
an ancient language in a bird-voice, the narrator explains the
ostensible miracle naturalistically as priestly machinations. Such
an explanation occurs frequently in *King Jesus* as well as *The
Nazarene Gospel Restored*. The same sort of rational explanation
of myth and folk belief is applied in "The Sibyl," where what
is explained and poetically utilized is the Celtic legend of the
Hounds of Hell or Gabriel Hounds whose origin is found "in the
strange noise made by the passage of flocks of wild geese or
swans." The centrality of the same hounds and explanation in
*The White Goddess* clearly testifies to the early beginnings of
Graves's interest in the world of myth.

Other poems in *Whipperginny* not only bear out the extent of
this interest but set it even more firmly in an anthropological and
comparative religion context at least part of which is clearly
provided by *The Golden Bough*. In "On the Poet's Birth" we
find both a more deliberately comparativist use of myth and an
unequivocal anticipation of the core of *The White Goddess*. The
poet has many fathers but only the mother is important, for as
she says to him, "acknowledge only me, be this enough, / For
such as worship after shall be told / A white dove sired you or a
rain of gold." The presence of Danae and Aphrodite and perhaps
the Christian Holy Ghost as well as Zeus and Perseus establishes
both the divinity and religious obligations of poetry and also
Graves's growing inclination to follow Frazer's practice of
creating a metamyth, as it were, out of several myths through
studying their comparative features.[31] Thus, the White Goddess

31. An interesting glimpse of the development of Graves's mythopoeic perspective is
provided by this poem. It suggests that the poet who worships the mother goddess is Perseus,
while in *The White Goddess*, pp. 540-41, Perseus is regarded as her chief antagonist.

and the sacrificial king have been criticized on substantially the same grounds of evidence and historical accuracy. But in point of fact both Frazer and Graves have clearly been providing not so much anthropological fact as poetic metaphors.

Facing "On the Poet's Birth" in the collection is "The Avengers." It perhaps even more dramatically points up the poet's early involvement with topics that come to fruition in *The White Goddess* as well as the hints concerning them that he derived from *The Golden Bough*. In this poem is the genesis of the second chapter of *The White Goddess*, for in six stanzas it details a battle between the trees of the South and East, who inaugurated the struggle, and those of the North and West. Among those mentioned are the quince, the briar-rose, the ivy, the oak, the ash, and the palm. All figure prominently in the nature symbolism of the central figure of *The White Goddess*. Frazer following Wilhelm Mannhardt paid substantial attention to the mythological significance of vegetation and so contributed substantially both to Graves's perspective and materials. Yet it is in the response of the northern trees to the attack of engraftment that *The Golden Bough* shows through most vividly. For,

> Then mistletoe, of gods not the least,
> Kindler of warfare since the Flood,
> Against green things of South and East
> Voices the vengeance of our blood.

Regardless of the poet's botanical knowledge, it is doubtful whether the parasitic nature of the plant could have afforded such a description without benefit of Frazer's researches. Not only is the mistletoe ultimately linked with the golden bough of antiquity itself by Frazer, but its extensive worship from Britain and the Druids to Japan as chronicled by Frazer provides a substantial warrant for likening it to a major deity.[32] Similarly, its reputation for indestructibility and its capacity for conferring

32. In *The White Goddess*, p. 56, it is connected with the old king as a phallic emblem. No such connotations appear in "The Avengers" (*Golden Bough*, 2:358, 362; 9:76 ff.).

invulnerability, which Frazer traces exhaustively, make it ideal for leading the counterattack against the forces of Mediterranean vegetation.[33] And, of course, as an ancient "kindler of warfare," it invokes the myth of Balder, a figure whose ritual Frazer explores elaborately in the final two volumes of *The Golden Bough*.

Despite the vigor of the assault led by the mistletoe, the poem closes on the failure of the West to halt its being overrun and imprisoned by eastern vegetation. Some of the latter, such as the quince, Graves in *The White Goddess* later identifies with Mediterranean worship of the woman and fertility:

> For bloom of quince yet caps the may,
> The briar is held by Sharon's rose,
> Monsters of thought through earth we stray,
> And how remission comes, God knows.[34]

Thus, like *The Golden Bough*, the poem stresses the mythic defeat or death rather than victory or life. It is much later that Graves finds the answer to the last line when he learns the true nature of the quince and its symbolism. Then he capitulates to the power of that great female figure, the wife-mother, who tells him in "On the Poet's Birth," "Acknowledge only me, be this enough."

Two of the major themes in *The Golden Bough* are vegetative fertility and human sexuality or, as Frazer has it, the preservation and perpetuation of mankind. The former has been seen to underlie "The Avengers." A perhaps even more explicit use of Frazer's anthropological materials in exploring the theme of sexuality appears in "The Snake and the Bull." In predominantly eight-line stanzas of tetrameter couplets, a first person narrator

---

33. *Golden Bough*, 9:79, 94.

34. This East-West struggle may owe something to *The Golden Bough* for Frazer stresses the movement of the great Asiatic fertility religions westward into Europe as they transform into Christianity (see 4:250, 298-312). Here Graves seems to regard the defeat of the West as regrettable whereas in *The White Goddess* it is western Christianity which has destroyed or driven underground the worship of the fertility goddess and so becomes the villain in his eyes.

recounts his magical acquisition of sexual attraction from a wizard namesake; his terror when Fesse, the ape god and "avenger of misuses by man / Of lust that by his art began," ambushes his companion; his flight and concealment in a world of ascetic chastity and intellectual sublimation; and the sudden flaring up of sexuality in the midst of astronomical speculation. Here, as in several of the poems just discussed, there is a firmness of language and a detachment of perspective that mark a substantial advance over Graves's earlier verse. It also attests to a toughening of his mind in which the astringencies of primitive barbarism and ironic tone exhibited by *The Golden Bough* may have had a salutary share. Certainly it seems to have contributed, if these poems are any evidence, substantially to that "new series of problems in religion, psychology and philosophy" which Graves announces in his foreword to *Whipperginny.*

Of a more specific order, however, are the Frazerian anthropological details which permeate the poem and make it one of the earliest and most explicitly aligned with *The Golden Bough.* Some of these details occur in the very first stanza:

> Snake Bull, my namesake, man of wrath,
> By no expense of knives or cloth,
> Only by work of muttered charms
> Could draw all woman to his arms;
> None whom he summoned might resist
> Nor none recall whom once he kissed
> And loosed them from his kiss, by whom
> This mother-shame had come.

As the poem develops, it becomes clear that both snake and bull are phallic emblems. They embody the twin modes of lust, assault, and deceit ("the Bull prancing, the Snake wriggling") and so perhaps hint at the differing roles of sexuality in pagan and Christian myths. Admittedly Frazer was not the first to make this identification, but it is virtually impossible not to feel that his stress upon the bull's typifying reproductive energy and its use in a variety of fertility rites figures in Graves's use of the image.[35]

The same is true of Frazer's noting such facts as that a snake was said to wound a girl at puberty, or that a Cretan fertility goddess was represented as snake-entwined, or that snakes were thought to have human wives and to father human beings.[36] To anyone interested in the new psychology associated with Freud, as Graves was at the time, Frazer's information would serve as striking confirmation of what might otherwise have seemed the highly dubious speculations of dream symbolism. The anthropological ambiance of these images is also strengthened by the narrator's namesake being a magician who, like those of Frazer, was both unscrupulous and capable of imposing his will on others through the exercise of spells. His capacity to make his women forget "by whom / This mother-shame had come" suggests too that Graves has crossed Frazer's account of magic with his discussions of the Asiatic custom of sacred prostitution in which the woman consorts with strangers and so calls the resultant offspring children of the god whom she is serving as a priestess.[37] And in the next stanza the points in *The Golden Bough* about personal names being regarded as a vital part and source of power of the individual and hence their being tabooed appear as the ground of Snake Bull's magic: "The power of his compelling flame / Was bound in virtue of our name."

Such power of sensual arousal is quickly abandoned, however, when Fesse ambushes the narrator's mentor. His fate, death by strangulation and crushing, is both naturalistic and, according to Frazer, appropriate to criminals.[38] More suggestive of *The Golden Bough*, however, are "the tree-top rites" from which the narrator flees without observing them. His last glimpse of his namesake is "Up through the air I saw him swung / To bridal bowers with red flowers hung." In this there is an ironic interweaving of the Adonis myth, Frazer's hanged god, and Jane

35.  *Golden Bough*, 5:36 ff.
36.  Ibid., 3:242, 243; 7:237.
37.  Ibid., 5:68.
38.  Ibid., 3:242-243; 9:252-253.

Harrison's point about the indistinguishability of Greek death and marriage rituals. To escape a similar fate the narrator not only flees but also performs a number of the primitive rituals described by Frazer. To escape a vengeful supernatural power like the ape god one must become another person and to this end the narrator directs his terrified attention with a scrupulous anthropological nicety:

> Cast off the livery of my clan,
> Over unlawful hills I ran,
> I soiled me with forbidden earth.
> In nakedness of second birth
> I scorched away the Snake's red eyes
> Tattooed for name about my thighs,
> And slew the Sacred Bull oppressed
> With passion on my breast.

Rituals of divestiture, rebirth, and sacrifice and the observation and breaking of taboos are borrowed from *The Golden Bough* and modulated into a definition of metamorphosis that charts the range of human reactions to terror.

Following these observances, the narrator finds himself in a new world and part of a new tribe whose customs and beliefs are the reverse of those in his former life. The women are Amazons who are indifferent to sexuality and maternity. The men are neither warriors or hunters but scholars whose devotion to astronomy recalls the Babylonian stargazers described by *The Golden Bough*.[39] Indeed, they are defined wholly negatively in terms of their divergence from the societies presented by Frazer:

> Possessions they have none, nor schools
> For tribal duties, nor close rules,
> No gods, no rites, no totem beasts,
> No friendships, no love feasts.

39. Ibid., 9:326. Cf. Yeats's "Two Songs from a Play."

The crux of the narrator's aspiration, which he feels he has achieved, is to be "quit, as they, of gong-roused lust." In such a heavily anthropological context as the whole poem provides, this last phrase seems inspired by Frazer's account of the bronze gongs of Dodona, the sanctuary of Zeus and his old wife Dione.[40]

Significantly enough, the fertility figures of *The Golden Bough* reassert themselves just as the narrator feels he has willed his conquest over sexuality. The Snake and the Bull burst forth into his consciousness with contempt and retribution for him who thought he could ever subdue the human sexual instinct:

> With desolating fire for one
> Who thought the Serpent's days were done,
> And girlish titterings from the trees
> Loosen my firm knees.

The "desolating fire" conveys the fact of his failure, the impossibility of success in such an endeavor, and the anguish of the arousal of feared and unwanted sensuality. In short, the narrator is the first of Graves's poetic personae to reap the bitter reward of slighting the orgiastic fertility goddess from whom all benefits flow including that of poetic inspiration.

By this time it is clear that Graves has started to take a substantial interest in the kind of mythology and anthropology so prominent in the pages of *The Golden Bough*. The strength of that interest can be well assessed by reference to *Mockbeggar Hall*, a collection that appeared the year after *Whipperginny* in 1924. This volume marks a radical extension of the interest in philosophical problems announced in *Whipperginny*. Now Graves, under the influence of an Indian friend at Oxford, is consumed by the subtle speculative abstractions of formal metaphysics. Yet despite this shift of interest, several of the

---

40. Ibid., 2:358 ff. In view of Graves's detailed knowledge of comparative mythology, it is possible he is here drawing also on A. B. Cook's *Zeus*, 3 vols. (Cambridge: Cambridge University Press, 1914-1940), which contains a more extensive discussion of Dodona than does *The Golden Bough*.

poems testify to Graves's continuing attention to primitive man, his magic and his religion as well as to the larger issue of the nature of myth itself. "Witches," for instance, shows a knowledge of their organization and practices, which similar to that later exhibited by Margaret Murray is a combination of reading in English Renaissance sources and imaginative extrapolation from those sources.[41] In the poem witches are linked to lovers as a symbol of states that defy empirical observation. The interesting thematic feature of this poem is Graves's argument that magic is real and true just as love is and that lack of belief in either is a sign of limited intelligence which brings its own punishment. This is not to say that he views magic in the manner of Aleister Crowley, of Charles Williams, or even William Butler Yeats. Rather magic seems to be associated with individually and personally induced imaginative experiences, with the mind's capacity to invent or remember situations that it is not now witnessing.

From this it is but a matter of increasing scope to the idea developed in "Antigonus: An Eclogue" that history and science are both tools to be manipulated for effect—a notion made more explicit in *Poetic Unreason* when he suggests that history is not an unchanging mirror image of some phase of life but has an identity distinct from that which it is a history of. The analogy he uses is the difference between dreaming and falling asleep, the former being history. As a result, history is a matter of interpreting material according to certain emotional formulae.[42] Such a position obviously helps explain the genesis and perhaps the rationale for Graves's later very cavalier way with conventional historical views in novels like *Wife to Mr. Milton* and *Homer's Daughter* as well as in ostensibly scholarly researches like *The White Goddess* and *The Nazarene Gospel Restored* or *Adam's Rib*.

Indeed, "Antigonus" contains a passage which is Graves's

---

41. In a note, *Mockbeggar Hall* (London: Hogarth Press, 1924), p. 24, Graves identifies one of his sources as *A True Discourse of the Apprehension of Sundry Witches lately taken in Scotland, 1591*.

42. *Poetic Unreason*, p. 156.

earliest statement on the relation of myth to other intellectual formulations like history and science:

JAMES.  Is there much fun in forging history?
          Nothing you write can ever alter facts.
JOHN.  When you say "history," what does that imply?
          The logical or the psychological?
          Logical? but there's history that refers
          To another context with new premises
          Not bound by challenge of empiric proof.
          One day this history may become supreme
          As your empiric kind succeeded myth,
          And then who'll be the forger, you or I?
JAMES.  John, I don't follow you: it sounds like nonsense.
          I can't believe you mean half what you say.
          Must we revert to myth?
JOHN.               No, not to myth
          In the dimmer sense, but a new form of myth
          Alert, with both eyes open, self-aware—
          This is my point, the past is always past
          And what the present calls past history
          Springing new, capricious, unforeseeable
          Not pinned to this or that structure of thought;
          Then what the structural classification
          Of Bruce and Spider, Washington and Hatchet,
          Alfred and Cakes, may prove in time to come,
          Or how such tales may alter in essentials
          By new research in one vein or the next,
          Do you dare prophesy?

Here we can see Graves drawing on Frazer's evolutionary idea of successive ages culminating in the scientific (Frazer suggested a sequence of magic-religion-science) and adding to it his own sense, shared by many in the twenties as well as more recently, that "a new form of myth" was necessary and about to appear. In a sense, this view has analogies with what I. A. Richards calls the theory of the projective imagination in that it conceives of all forms of intellectual organization including science and religions as mythical.[43] And insofar as myths were vulgarly regarded as primitive superstitions by many people, the view may owe something to *Psyche's Task* in which Frazer suggests that superstitions or factual falsehoods may nevertheless be extremely useful to man.

The connections between "Antigonus: An Eclogue" and "Mock Beggar Hall" are essentially twofold. In both, Graves employs a dialogue between a poet and an antithetical mind, in one case a literary historian and in the other a philosopher. What is important here is that it is the poet who is seeking for a viable alternative to these established and respectable positions. He does so by turning to myth both in abstract terms and in concrete imagery. It is this reliance on myth that forms the second link between these two works. Though both are dialogues or dramatic in manner, they approach myth differently. The poet of "Antigonus" looks for a new form of myth which his version of the Urtale of Antigonus and the bear, found in *The Winter's Tale,* seems to equate with the poetic imagination and its ability to reorder narratives into new tales. The poet in "Mock Beggar Hall" finds "poetry and dreams are closely allied and sometimes identical" and recounts a new poem that employs specific mythic elements from the past. Thus, the subtitle "A Progression" refers to a haunted house that in the past has been variously a synogogue, a church, and a shrine to Venus. In focusing on this kind of architectural archaeology, Graves is taking the same tack as Frazer who points out that the Vatican was formerly the site for the worship of Cybele and Attis.[44] And by viewing the historical succession of pagan, Jewish, and Christian religions as a struggle between the living and "their ghostly predecessors"

---

43. I. A. Richards, *Coleridge on Imagination* (London: Routledge & Kegan Paul, 1934), pp. 176-77. Interestingly enough, in the same chapter (p. 181), Richards quotes F. H. Bradley as saying " 'human beings cannot get on without mythology.' " Though Bradleyan idealism was on the wane at Oxford by 1918, one may wonder what Graves's philosophizing owes to it during this period.

44. *Golden Bough,* 5:275 ff.

in which the latter harass and terrify their successors, Graves seems to adapt Frazer's theory about fear being the source of religion and the worship of the dead to his own comparative view of the relation between religions. The ghosts of the dead of primitive tribesmen are transformed into historically prior religions in order to make an ironic point about the fate and futility of religious dogmatism. And matching these larger thematic borrowings is Graves's explicitly anthropological interest when he searches for the antecedents of the Romans' worship of Venus:

> And these Romans
> Had they no strange incursions at their shrine
> Of Druid knives and basket-sacrifices
> Breaking the sacred raptures of the kiss?
> Was not their temple founded here to mask
> The lopped oakgrove of aboriginal gods?

He singles out in his diction—"knives," "sacrifices," "oakgrove" —the very features most stressed by Frazer in his discussions of the Druids, and then caps the similarity with "aboriginal" whose anthropological coloring reflects *The Golden Bough*'s comparative attempts to trace parallels in the rites of Australian aborigines, Celtic Druids, and classical worshippers at the Arician grove.

From here on, with the exception of one reference to a prophetic Ogham verse, the poem veers away from comparative religion into a dialectical exploration of comparative political and moral philosophy, though the two emphases are ostensibly linked by the poem's being described in the prose portions of the narrative as a gradually broadening allegory. This, coupled with the dabbling in Elizabethan political allegory in the manner of Lilian Winstanley in "Antigonus," suggests that one of Graves's first poetic reactions to anthropology and *The Golden Bough* was to use its materials—themes and images—in framing allegorical poems that seek to explore philosophical problems.

Subsequently he was to deepen his perception of the character of myth. It ceased to be merely ancient tales reflecting outmoded beliefs and stood revealed as immemorial records of man's enduring efforts to project his deepest sense of reverence into his immediate, temporal, sociopolitical context. At the same time, he was to move poetically from the early nursery tales and ballads through poems that are both longer and variously analytic or allegorical to dramatic lyrics. The characteristic Gravesian poem is a tautly controlled rendering of a facet of the relations of man and woman so that even the most commonplace events and moods share in the mythic pattern of attraction, struggle, and defeat, of birth, life, and death. And if the technical modulations in his verse can be ascribed to the evolution of his own poetic temperament as well as the tutelage of Laura Riding, the thematic deepening similarly derives from his acquisition of an encyclopedic familiarity with the authorities of comparative religion among whom Frazer was preeminent.

CHAPTER II

# The White Goddess
# and King Jesus

Up to this point the focus has been on establishing Graves's early acquaintance with *The Golden Bough* and the world of anthropology and myth generally while at the same time suggesting some of Graves's interests which would have made him particularly receptive to the world of Frazer and his cohorts. It is clear that Graves did indeed have a measure of anthropological knowledge quite early in his career. Its full poetic value, however, was not recognized, largely because Graves had not yet found his appropriate form or poetic theory that would fully release his imagination. Nevertheless, he continued to employ the materials of myth, legend, and folklore in both poetry and prose with increasing knowledge and sureness until the middle 1940s when he began to formulate his theory of the White Goddess, which has dominated his mind ever since. There would perhaps be some value in tracing the evolution of Graves's command of poetic myth. Nevertheless, a more coherent view is likely to emerge if we abandon the chronological approach for the thematic. In this way we will be able to get a detailed view of precisely what the dominant mythic motifs are and how they interrelate under the rubric of his overriding theory about the nature of myth and poetry. By so doing we will also be subscribing to what seems to be Graves's own preference in the matter. For as early as 1938, in the preface to his *Collected Poems* of that year, he suggested that the poems were placed in numbered sections in the volume because they revealed a psychological and thematic development. And while the poems do possess a rough kind of chronological order, as Graves says, their dominant order seems to be thematic. The same order has for the most part been preserved in the various *Collected Poems* that have appeared since, though, of course, with the addition of new sections as needed.

In tracing the lineaments of the mature Graves's basic myth-motif and its relation to *The Golden Bough*, two complementary works stand out. These are *The White Goddess* and *King Jesus*, which first appeared around the same time and which are far more important in this respect than *Hercules, My Shipmate*, the work whose research Graves claims first made him aware of the ubiquity of the White Goddess.[1] Actually his preparations for a full-scale study of myth antedate the Hercules novel by at least ten years and probably longer. Thus, to look at his first novels *I, Claudius* and *Claudius the God* is to see the measure of his interest in the worlds explored by Frazer and others. The first of these novels contains no explicit references to *The Golden Bough* or its themes and seems to be a quite ordinary historical novel drawing on classical sources. Still, it does suggest unequivocally that history is the record of infamy and the historian a dispassionate chronicler. This same attitude is one that dominates much of *The Golden Bough* particularly when it discusses the rise of the priest-king to a position of power or the efforts of organized religions to hold and extend their power.

In its sequel, published in the same year, Graves is more explicit about his anthropological knowledge. He says, for instance, that his ideas about British Druidism were aided by "borrowings from archaeological works, from ancient Celtic literature and from accounts of modern megalithic culture in the New Hebrides, where the dolmen and menhir are still ceremoniously used."[2] Among the ideas discussed in the course of the novel are those dealing with rituals for producing rain, the importance of the oak and mistletoe in primitive religions, the

---

1. See Graves, *Five Pens in Hand* (New York: Doubleday, 1958), pp. 55-72, and Day, *Swifter Than Reason*, pp. 154-56.
2. Graves, *Claudius the God* (New York: Harrison Smith and Robert Haas, 1935), p. 6.

nature of the Saturnalia, the practice of women worshippers having sexual intercourse with their gods, the cult of Cybele with its eunuch priests, and the centrality of Jesus' resurrection and reappearance to the success of Christianity.[3] As he himself avers, Graves likely drew on a number of sources for his information. It is, however, also true that all of these points are made, sometimes in copious detail, in *The Golden Bough*. And though he has not yet evolved the White Goddess Graves does have Claudius use the cult of Cybele, the great orgiastic fertility goddess of Phrygia, as the basis for a kind of comparative study of religion from the standpoint of a practical politician and ruler. Similar adumbrations of the motifs of *The White Goddess* emerge in the notion of the god Osiris as a triple figure, in a human being annually serving as the god's representative and having the right to all human pleasures before being sacrificed, and in the importance attached to the number thirteen, as well as the significance of natural analogies as argumentative support and a method of reasoning. In *Claudius the God* these have become the triple goddess, her sacrificial consort, the ancient lunar year, and the book's essential logic respectively.

While *Hercules, My Shipmate* shows a number of these developments as full blown and adds others, such as the matriarchal stress, it can be bypassed in favor of *The White Goddess* if only because it is the latter book which has been most influential and which perhaps best sums up Graves's approach to myth and anthropology. Trying to summarize the leading concerns of a book that at first glance is as maddening as Yeats's *A Vision* is difficult. Yet in a general sense it is possible to isolate three recurring strands which stand out as central. These are the nature of poetry and modes of human thought, the myth of the White Goddess and her consort, and what might be called the religious symbolism of language. Of these it is obviously the second that is most closely linked with *The Golden Bough*, though the others have affinities too through their connection with the goddess and her lover.

3. Ibid., pp. 227, 290, 295, 302, 391, 394, 452.

Briefly put, Graves argues that certain medieval Welsh poems, notably "The Battle of the Trees" and "The Tale of Taliesin" from *The Red Book of Hergest,* were deliberately confused so that their real significance—a symbolic and arcane statement of the name of the transcendent God—would not be detected by the authorities of the Christian church. The ultimate reason for the church's hostility is not only that the God named is a pagan one but, says Graves, that it is the Great Mother goddess of the original matriarchal age. She is hated and feared by those of the patriarchal age who have replaced her, for she embodies the mysteries of fertility and generation and demands man's "spiritual and sexual homage." To this they have retorted by exalting patrilinear institutions and reason or logic, both of which are calculated to expunge the power of the goddess.

Actually, the Welsh poems and their esoteric significance are but the vehicle on which Graves mounts his general thesis. He argues that the original language of poetry employed the grammar and vocabulary of myth, which in turn was based on a close knowledge and observation of the seasons and the various forms of vegetative life. This language was devoted to invoking, celebrating, and otherwise worshipping the primitive moon-goddess who is the true poet's true muse. This sense of the nature and function of myth was gradually driven underground where it survived in such disparate locations as the mystery cults at Eleusis, the ancient Celtic schools for poets, and the covens of witches in western Europe. But today there is no organized, disciplined study or worship of either the goddess or her poetic mode. Instead there is industrialism, patriarchalism, and classical poetry celebrating Apollo and reason, all enemies of the White Goddess and true poetry. Thus Graves claims to be concerned with rediscovering and expounding the lost rudiments of the magical principles that underlay the original forms of European poetic lore. In so doing, he will, he feels, be providing a nucleus of poetic education for those aspiring poets who are truly dedicated and prepared to make a total commitment to the craft of poetry.

Central to this education is the understanding of the true nature of poetic theme. Graves suggests that the determination of the true theme depends on the reaction of the reader, a fact which suggests the residual effects of his early involvement with psychoanalysis and W. H. R. Rivers. When a poem is perfectly rendering the "single yet infinitely variable Theme," the reader experiences "a strange feeling, between delight and horror." [4] And yet one is not confined to the psychological determination. Graves also suggests a descriptive characterization of the theme:

> The Theme, briefly, is the antique story, which falls into thirteen chapters and an epilogue, of the birth, life, death and resurrection of the God of the Waxing Year; the central chapters concern the God's losing battle with the God of the Waning Year for love of the capricious and all-powerful Threefold Goddess, their mother, bride and layer-out. The poet identifies himself with the God of the Waxing Year and his Muse with the Goddess; the rival is his blood-brother, his other self, his weird. [5]

In short, the true poetic theme, the only real one for the serious poet, is life and death mediated by love whose archetypal form is the myth of the White Goddess. In it she imperiously and arbitrarily chooses a lover, bestows her favors on him, has a child by him, and then puts him to death before taking another lover.

These two ways of characterizing the theme of poetry combine shrewdly in Graves's poetic. The psychological explanation in terms of reader reaction suggests that whatever arouses the feeling compounded of delight and horror is a version of the theme. When this is taken in conjunction with the description of the theme in terms of the goddess and her consort, it becomes clear how Graves's mythopoeic interests merge with his fascination with contemporary concerns such as celebrating the love between individual human beings. For when the reader responds

4. *The White Goddess*, p. 8.
5. Ibid., p. 11.

with delight and horror, he is, Graves can claim, responding to the powers of the goddess. By the same token, those poems that deal more explicitly with mythic topics already have defined for them the kind of response they should arouse so that in a sense Graves is very subtly preconditioning the audience. At the same time, of course, should such poems not arouse such a response, then this can be taken as evidence that while the subject is appropriate the treatment is not.

In this way he has a check against automatically assuming that the mythological poem is a good one, and at the same time he extends the notion of the range of poetic myth. For if the effect is the same and due to the same cause, then poems ostensibly personal and contemporary in subject are also aspects of the myth of the goddess and her lover. The effect of this is to suggest that the distinction frequently drawn between Graves's mythic poems and his others is misplaced; they really all form part of one infinitely various and developing story. What Graves is doing, then, is to restore to "myth" not only its original function as "grave records of ancient religious customs and events" [6] but also a good deal of its original form and meaning as a word. That is, his contemporary poems dramatize for us the fact that the original sense of the word *myth* was simply that of *story*, and stories of human situations, emotions, and events are precisely what his poems supply in abundance.

## II

Since this study does not purport to be a full-scale examination of Graves's poetry, this and similar matters must be set to one side. Nor can we even hope to examine in anything like the detail it demands *The White Goddess* itself. The central issue is to what extent that book is shaped by *The Golden Bough* and in what distinctive ways. It has been shown that Graves exhibited an early and considerable poetic interest in anthropology and comparative religion. It might be thought, however, that a work that deals with medieval Welsh poems, Celtic Ogham alphabets,

6. Ibid., p. x.

Essene beliefs, and biblical symbology is one that has left the relative sobriety of *The Golden Bough* for headier areas of exploration. Even a casual reading (if such a thing is possible) of *The White Goddess* will dispel this notion. In all there are approximately twenty explicit references or quotations from Frazer as well as several others to Jane Harrison.[7] In addition there are almost thirty other passages which can with varying degrees of confidence be regarded as using *The Golden Bough* or other of Frazer's works as sources for the ideas advanced or as evidence or authority for the opinions expressed.[8]

While such elementary statistics do not themselves establish the centrality of Frazer to Graves's study of myth, they do count for something. If nothing else they document both Graves's conversancy with *The Golden Bough* and his willingness to draw on it. But they do more. The tenor of his remarks about Frazer have a threefold emphasis. First, as he suggests in his interpretation of the myth of Uranus-Cronus-Zeus as "the annual supplanting of the old oak-king by his successor,[9] . . . the theory of Frazer's *Golden Bough* is familiar enough to make this point unnecessary to elaborate at length."[10] Second, he assumes the essential correctness of many of Frazer's interpretations; for example, he draws directly on *The Golden Bough*'s discussion of the corn spirit as an animal to support his claim that cat, pig, and wolf were particularly sacred to the Celtic goddess Cerridwen, the moon-goddess in her aspect as death-goddess.[11] At the same time, Graves is not slavishly reliant on Frazer, and this takes us to the third aspect of his remarks about Frazer.

Running through *The White Goddess* is an attitude toward Frazer which can best be described as the critical impatience of a descendant. This is best typified by two instances. In the first,

---

7. Ibid., pp. 56, 58, 129-30, 135, 166, 181, 183, 186, 224 n. 1, 234, 246, 259, 283, 315-16, 356, 407, 408 and n. 1, 415, 442, 464, 526-27.
8. Ibid., pp. 35, 51, 55-56, 59, 123, 127, 132, 159, 178, 220, 228, 268, 298, 312 n. 6, 334, 344, 346, 349, 354, 369, 427, 449, 467, 492, 496, 532.
9. Ibid., p. 55.
10. Ibid., p. 56; see also p. 181.
11. Ibid., p. 234; cf. *Golden Bough*, 7:274.

after mentioning Frazer's point about the similarity of words for *door* in Indo-European languages, Graves then goes on to say that "as usual, however, he [Frazer] does not press his argument far enough." [12] The second instance is a more extended criticism of Frazer for having preserved his academic position by exercising considerable discretion in discussing the primitive and pagan origins of Christianity. As Graves puts it, Frazer retained his position "by carefully and methodically sailing all around his dangerous subject, as if charting the coastline of a forbidden island without actually committing himself to a declaration that it existed." [13] Like Lawrence, Graves is unwilling to use Frazer and *The Golden Bough* without also affirming his independence. Indeed, there is more than a suggestion in his criticisms of Frazer that he is rebuking Frazer less for his views than for his not having a temperament and attitude more like that of Robert Graves. After *The White Goddess* and *The Nazarene Gospel Restored*, no one is likely to accuse Graves of not having carried his argument far enough or of not stating his position unequivocally.

From these three points of emphasis—familiarity, correctness, and incompleteness—we can chart with remarkable accuracy the character of Graves's use of *The Golden Bough*. Because he assumes Frazer's theories are well known, Graves mentions them without elaborating on them in detail. And because he thinks many of Frazer's individual statements and observations are undeniably true, he cites or alludes to them for corroboration of his own vastly more elaborate and ingenious theories. As a result there is considerably more use of points drawn from *The Golden Bough* than there is exposition of its central theses. At the same time, since his own views about the nature and dis-

12. *The White Goddess*, p. 183; cf. pp. 56, 130. In the case of the last example, Graves is less than just to Frazer, for Frazer makes precisely the point he is accused of not making (*Golden Bough*, 5:45-47). In addition, Graves's own quotation from Frazer, pp. 129-30, is inaccurate in two particulars. Both these points testify less to Graves's ignorance of *The Golden Bough* than to the casualness of his scholarship.
13. *The White Goddess*, p. 259; cf. Graves, *Occupation: Writer* (New York: Creative Age, 1950), pp. 42-43.

semination of myths are more involved and speculative than those of Frazer, and since he is not a professional scholar but rather a gifted amateur—a unique cross between Lord Raglan and Ezra Pound—he feels temperamentally impelled to declare the inadequacies of the author of *The Golden Bough*.

Partially qualifying these strictures, however, is the substantial evidence of his extensive knowledge of Frazer's works. In *The White Goddess* alone Graves's quotations from or allusions to *The Golden Bough* range from early volumes like *Taboo and the Perils of the Soul* to the very last ones entitled *Balder the Beautiful*.[14] Other works of Frazer that he has drawn on here or elsewhere are *Totemism and Exogamy*, *Folk-Lore in the Old Testament*, the editions of Apollodorus's *Bibliotheca*, Ovid's *Fasti*, and Pausanias's *Graeciae Descriptio*.[15] And the probability is very great that he is well acquainted with still other lesser known works by Frazer, not only because of his intimate knowledge of *The Golden Bough* but also because of his awareness of many other authors in the field such as Bronislaw Malinowski, Jane Harrison, A. M. Hocart, Sir Flinders Petrie, Lord Raglan, A. B. Cook, W. H. R. Rivers, and Sir John Rhys.

In general terms we have seen the extent and kind of influence *The Golden Bough* exerted on Graves and *The White Goddess*. More specific examination, however, indicates that Frazer is not simply a source of evidence or a basis for extrapolations in *The White Goddess*. Actually, Graves's book is a kind of displacement and complication of the central themes of *The Golden Bough*. The centrality of the goddess and her consort to Graves's thesis is obvious, but it is precisely here in this myth that Graves is most receptive to Frazer's impact. In *The Golden Bough* Frazer focuses the central phenomenon in the development of

---

14. See, e.g., his quotation from Frazer, pp. 129-30, and his reference to *The Golden Bough*'s treatment of the need-fire ceremony, p. 464.

15. *The White Goddess*, pp. 59, 224 n. 1, 230-31, 407-8 and n. 1; *Hercules, My Shipmate* (New York: Creative Age, 1945), p. 460; *King Jesus*, 5th ed. (London: Cassell, 1960), pp. 51, 67, 202-3, 206, 216. It is likely that Graves has connected Frazer's *The Worship of Nature* (London: Macmillan, 1926), also, particularly for its treatment of sun worship. For his possible acquaintance with Frazer's *Belief in Immortality*, see p. 12 n. 30, above.

man's religious consciousness. Thus, while he gives due attention to Isis, Ishtar, Aphrodite, and the others, the bulk of his discussion centers on gods like Adonis, Attis, Osiris, and Balder, who suffer the critical experience of sacrificial death and whose restoration to the full vigor of life is essential to the perpetuation of their worshippers. For the most part, their consorts are cast in the secondary role of compliant lovers and devoted mourners who, like Isis, wander desolate over the earth after his death and ultimately have their faithfulness rewarded by the god's revival and triumph over his adversary and death.

In essence, Graves deals with the same myths but from an inverted perspective: he concentrates on the goddess as the central figure responsible for the fertility and flourishing of all living things. In this he echoes Frazer's stress upon such Asiatic mother goddesses as the personification of all reproductive energies in nature. At the same time, what allows him to do so with such ease is the copious evidence provided by Frazer that originally the goddess was more important than her spouse. *The Golden Bough* explains this in, among other places, a crucial chapter entitled "Mother-Kin and Mother Goddesses." This chapter is of vital importance in pointing up Graves's response to Frazer. The latter says that the goddess's superiority over the god is best explained "as the result of a social system in which maternity counted for more than paternity, descent being traced and property handed down through women rather than through men." [16]

Graves accepts this view but extends it to mean that originally women as representatives or embodiments of the goddess were politically preeminent and ruled society.[17] Such a thesis flatly contradicts Frazer's argument that mother-kin or the custom of matrilineal descent does not imply that the government is in the hands of women. Indeed, Frazer goes so far as to say that "the theory that under a system of mother-kin the women rule the men and set up goddesses for them to worship is so improbable

16. *Golden Bough*, 6:202.
17. While this is the general drift of *The White Goddess*, the clearest statement of this view and of Graves's notion of the stages society has traversed historically is in his *Greek Myths*, 2 vols. (Baltimore: Penguin, 1955), 1:ii.

in itself, and so contrary to experience, that it scarcely deserves the serious attention which it appears to have received." [18] The explanation for this divergence in views is perhaps that Graves is concerned with pushing his argument further than Frazer. The latter argues that all available evidence points away from the idea of a thoroughgoing matriarchy, while Graves feels that there was an earlier stage in society when such a mode of organization existed.

In this, Graves is possibly indebted to Laura Riding, though not in the fashion some critics have suggested. At one point in *Claudius the God* he acknowledges her aid on matters of what he calls "literary congruity," [19] by which he means logical consistency applied to the construction of literary works. It is, quite possibly, this sense of literary congruity that impels him to infer a matriarchal state from the considerable evidence for the preeminence of goddesses in certain societies at certain periods in history. The neatness of this hypothesis also squares with Graves's penchant for standing accepted views of historical incidents on their heads, as he has in such novels as *Sergeant Lamb's America* and *Wife to Mr. Milton*. Frequently he shows that the truth about a character or event is not significantly different from but diametrically opposite to the received opinion.

If the White Goddess is Frazer's fertility goddesses exalted in her religious centrality, her character also owes a good deal to the same personages. Actually what Graves has done is to make a composite goddess out of those figures discussed by Frazer. He augments Frazer's remarks with information from other sources, both ancient and modern, as well as with his own speculative inferences based on highly imaginative readings of the available documents and evidence. Thus, *The Golden Bough* stresses the vegetative aspect of these goddesses, their human embodiment of that form of fertility on which primitive peoples depended for their sustenance. Frazer traces in considerable

---

18. *Golden Bough*, 6:211-12. Cf. ibid., 2:271 n. 2. See also Henry Bamford Parkes, *Gods and Men* (London: Routledge & Kegan Paul, 1960), p. 27 n. 1.
19. *Claudius the God*, p. 6.

detail the precise plants, trees, and flowers held sacred to the individual goddesses. Graves does the same thing when he makes the White Goddess a goddess of trees and specifies which ones are linked with the goddesses of various peoples. His linking of the Sumerian goddess Belili with the willow is of precisely the same order as Frazer's ascribing corn to Isis. And like Frazer he sees deities who have the same kinds of vegetation sacred to them as being identified with one another.

The chief difference is again one of degree. Frazer is content to link Isis, Ceres, and Demeter as corn goddesses and devoted wives and mothers. Graves goes beyond this to postulate a divine figure who embraces all the various forms of the fertility goddesses, from orgiastic tryrant to serene helpmate. It is she whom he calls the White Goddess. In so doing he carries the Frazerian comparative method a step beyond its use in *The Golden Bough*, though in a way that is inherent in its pages. Frazer orders the myths and rituals of the deities in a steady succession of chapters. Long before he is done this conveys to us an overwhelming sense of their similarity and of their all being in some sense versions of the same hopes, fears, and needs. The recurring pattern creates a perspective of identification which is also one of identity.

Graves does the same thing though more by direct assertion than indirection. Rhetorically his is the order of anticlimax whereas Frazer's is the order of climax. Thus, the White Goddess is a conceptual myth founded on ritual and functional similarities in deities whose worship is historically veridical. No one except Graves ever worshipped her though many peoples may have worshipped goddesses one of whose attributes was that of whiteness. In substance she holds the same position in Graves's thought as the Dying God does in Frazer's. The only difference is that Frazer, the professional scholar and historian, is content to regard his concept as just that while Graves is inclined to see in his a historical reality.

In the process of formulating this composite figure, Graves does more, however, than merely assemble an amalgam of the fertility goddesses discussed in *The Golden Bough*. He recognizes clearly that they possess contradictory and unreconcilable qualities. Isis and Astarte, for example, embody opposite poles of the female temperament and behavior. What he does is to present the White Goddess as a creature of almost infinitely metamorphic nature who changes her guises, roles, and qualities, as well as names. These changes are not capricious but rather correlated to the phases of the moon, the time of year, and the various functional relationships obtaining between her and man. In this way he is able to make her simultaneously a vital figure throughout the entirety of human life and also a single, enduring, archetypal creature. What is striking here, apart from the symmetrical ingenuity exercised by Graves in working out her paradigmatic development, is the extent to which material and clues for such an orientation are traceable to *The Golden Bough*.

As the human image of the changing moon, she has, according to Graves, the following pattern: "the New Moon is the white goddess of birth and growth; the Full moon, the red goddess of love and battle; the Old Moon the black goddess of death and divination." [20] Nowhere in *The Golden Bough* is there a comparably explicit statement of the moon pattern; Frazer does, however, devote considerable attention to the role of the moon in primitive religion. Included in his treatment are such points as the identification of certain goddesses and women with the moon, either in its new or harvest phases; the likening of the moon, in its waxing or waning phases, to a white cow and to "a coy or wanton maiden"; the primitive distinction between light and dark phases of the moon; and the correlation held to exist by many primitive peoples between human and lunar development.[21] What Graves does is to codify and sharpen these points of Frazer's so that a clear imaginative pattern emerges.

It is also possible that Frazer aids in the selection of color symbolism employed. The use of white and black is obvious and

20. *The White Goddess*, p. 61. This is not a rigidly adhered to use of color symbolism apparently, for on the preceding page Graves speaks of Cerridwen, the sow- and barley-goddess, as "the White Lady of Death and Inspiration" (p. 59).

21. *Golden Bough*, 2:128, 146; 4:73; 6:132, 138, 141, 144, 148; 9:140.

natural, but the ascription of red to the full moon is less so. In the passage just quoted Graves is altering Suidas's term *rose* and this obviously is the primary source in this particular instance. At the same time there is a curious parallel to this color symbolism in the final chapter of *The Golden Bough*. In the penultimate paragraph of his monumental study Frazer discusses what he calls the web of thought, the pattern human thought has revealed in the course of its development. He likens it to "a web woven of three different threads—the black thread of magic, the red thread of religion, and the white thread of science, if under science we may include those simple truths, drawn from observation of nature, of which men in all ages have possessed a store." [22] These concepts qua concepts may at first sight seem alien to the thought of *The White Goddess*, but when we look closely at the passage, its affinities with Graves's pattern increase. In both cases, black is associated with magic, divination being one form of it; white is connected with growth, though to be sure in somewhat different though still analogous senses; and red as emblematic of religion may well be thought to entail both love and battle. Also, the goddess who possesses these three forms often seems to represent for Graves the entire chameleonlike relationship obtaining between man and his environment. Thus, Frazer's web of thought is matched by a complex of fate and response that defines the destiny of man whatever the ground and character of his actions. The White Goddess is both the natural and psychological worlds in which the individual must live subject to forces other than his own untrammeled will.

The lunar trinity of the natural world has a parallel in the social world as well through which the functional relationships between goddess and man are defined. She also corresponds to what Graves considers as the three primary roles of woman, namely, maiden, mother, and old woman. The full complexity with which Graves sees her triple role is clear from the following passage:

22. Ibid., 9:308.

As Goddess of the Underworld she was concerned with Birth, Procreation and Death. As Goddess of the Earth she was concerned with the three seasons of Spring, Summer and Winter: she animated trees and plants and ruled all living creatures. As Goddess of the Sky she was the Moon in her three phases of New Moon, Full Moon and Waning Moon. This explains why from a triad she was so often enlarged to an ennead. But it must never be forgotten that the Triple Goddess, as worshipped for example at Stymphalus, was a personification of primitive woman—woman the creatress and destructress. As the New Moon or Spring she was girl; as the Full Moon or Summer she was woman; as the Old Moon or Winter she was hag.[23]

Though these roles are part of life itself, it is interesting to note the extent to which they are emphasized in *The Golden Bough*; it seems likely the pattern owes more than a little to Graves's steeping himself in Frazer's work. Particularly apposite here is the first of the two volumes called *Spirits of the Corn and of the Wild*. It deals at length with Demeter and Persephone and their relationship, with the preeminent role of women in agricultural rituals, and with the metamorphic and sacrificial character of corn spirits. Not only are Demeter and Persephone seen as mother and maiden respectively, but they are also regarded as successive forms of the same thing, the corn at different stages in its growth. By presenting a continuity of nature coupled with transformation of appearance and role, *The Golden Bough* gave him not only images of fertility but also the rationale with which to coalesce them into a unified emblem of female power viewed as a religious phenomenon. Graves even continues to exploit its vegetative emphasis when he remarks that the goddess was also worshipped "in her triple capacity of white raiser, red reaper and dark winnower of grain." [24] Similarly, though he is not wholly consistent in titling the roles, he follows Frazer in designating the youthful goddess as "maiden" and the aged

23. *The White Goddess*, p. 428.
24. Ibid., p. 62; cf. *The Greek Myths*, 1:92-93.

one as "hag." [25] Further aid for his symbolic schematizing is Frazer's information that the spring was called Persephone and the summer Aphrodite, while ceremonies connected with winter represented it as both aged and deformed, that is, as a hag.[26]

From the foregoing we have seen something of the way Graves links the White Goddess to temporal periods, both monthly and annual, lunar and solar. There is, however, another pattern of development that is at least partly temporal. It is a progression that represents biological and psychological rather than astronomical or vegetative reality. There are "five stations of the year, typified by the five petals of the Lotus-cup — Birth, Initiation, Marriage, Rest from Labour, and Death." [27] This explains, he says, why the apple has been given "such immense mythic importance" because "if an apple is halved cross-wise each half shows a five-pointed star in the centre, emblem of immortality, which represents the Goddess in her five stations from birth to death and back to birth again." [28] *The Golden Bough* has no such clear-cut delineation of seasonal or biological stages as this, it is true. Nevertheless, it contains much material to suggest this kind of pattern. All the stations save "Rest from Labour" are exhaustively explored in manifold dimensions by Frazer. The various rituals and beliefs associated with birth, initiation, marriage, and death help shape this pattern in Graves's thought.

Similarly, though the linking of the apple with the sequential movement of life itself is Graves's own, Frazer makes a number of points which bear out the apple's mythic importance. And these points may well have started Graves looking for an explana-

25. For some reason he studiously avoids calling the mature goddess *mother* as suggested in modern usage. The choice of *nymph* is hallowed by classical usage obviously, but Graves's choice may also have been triggered by Frazer's discussion of Egeria who, as a form of Diana, was credited with facilitating both female conception and delivery. See *Golden Bough*, 2:171-73.

26. Ibid., 6:41; 4:258; 10:116. The naming of the seasons occurs on the space of a single page, 6:41. Since the winter is called Cronus, this may suggest Graves's reason for the title "Crone." His familiarity with the Aphrodite-summer identification is clear from *The Greek Myths*, 1:71.

27. *The White Goddess*, p. 138.

28. Ibid., p. 277.

tion of its significance. Thus, he shows that it was a sacrificial offering to Hercules, whom Graves not only regards as "the most perplexing character in Classical mythology" but as the preeminent instance of the sacred king whose story is that of the ritual course of life itself.[29] It is Hercules who is seen to progress through the several stations described in the above passage. That the apple can be regarded as symbolizing the goddess may also have been suggested by its emblematic use at the festival of Diana in the summer, its employment as a fertility charm for barren women, its use in divination when sliced, and its tree serving as an index of the life expectancy of male children.[30] Even without detailed study it is clear from these items that the apple was symbolically identified with fertility, with birth, marriage, and death, which comprise three of Graves's five stations of the year.

Such a series of stages emphasizes, even as it orders, the metamorphoses undergone by the goddess both in the course of a year and in the life of the individual worshipper. It corresponds in large measure to the cyclical pattern that *The Golden Bough* enunciates for the dying and reviving god. Both possess a mysterious birth, marvellous experiences of multiple initiation including that of the sacred marriage with a divine woman, and death by accident or design from which there is a resurrection to renewed glory. This does not mean, however, that Graves's goddess is merely a female version of Frazer's deity. Rather, she is Frazer's fertility goddess who shares in the god's cyclic movement through annual stations but as originator and spectator, not participant. In Graves as in Frazer, "it is always the god rather than the goddess who comes to a sad end, and whose death is annually mourned." [31] For both, the divinity of the male lies in his capacity for resurrection, while that of the female stems from her immortality the proof of which is the continued existence of mankind.

29.  Ibid., p. 123; see also pp. 123-34; *The Greek Myths*, 2:88; *Golden Bough*, 8:95 n. 2.
30.  *Golden Bough*, 1:14, 16; 2:57; 10:238; 11:165.
31.  Ibid., 6:201.

According to Graves, the central functions of the goddess in relation to man are mother, wife or lover, and layer-out. The first two, as we have seen, are amply represented in *The Golden Bough*, where they probably provided Graves with the archetypes and images necessary to the creation of the White Goddess. The layer-out, however, is not nearly so prominent in Frazer's work. There seems to be no fully individualized goddess of the order of Persephone the maiden or Isis the wife-mother to lend significance to the one who prepares the body for burial. And yet if Graves is not simply filling out the sequence in logical fashion and recalling as do Lawrence and Joyce the folk custom of his youth, there is some material in *The Golden Bough* that might have proven stimulating. One of Frazer's central theses, heavily documented, is that fear of the dead played a prominent part in primitive life. So powerful and thoroughgoing was it that a number of taboos surrounded those persons who had come in contact with death or the dead. These taboos were of such stringency that the layer-out and other members of the burial party were "cut off from all intercourse and almost all communication with mankind." [32] Consequently, such individuals were reduced to the haglike state Graves equates with the death-goddess. In one of his typically graphic descriptions, Frazer presents a prototype of such persons:

> Clad in rags, daubed from head to foot with red ochre and stinking shark oil, always solitary and silent, generally old, haggard, and wizened, often half crazed, he might be seen sitting motionless all day apart from the common path or thoroughfare of the village, gazing with lack-lustre eyes on the busy doings in which he might never take a part. . . . at night, huddling his greasy tatters about him, he would crawl into some miserable lair of leaves and refuse, where, dirty, cold, and hungry, he passed, in broken ghost-haunted slumbers, a wretched night as a prelude to another wretched day.[33]

32. Ibid., 3:138.
33. Ibid., 3:139.

Admittedly such figures seem remote from Graves's layer-out, who is the human form of the death-goddess. Nevertheless, Frazer's account does focus on those elements of age, ugliness, insanity, and silence which epitomize the meeting with the death-goddess. Transposed to the female, they might well define her appearance for Graves. Her loathsome and ferocious nature Graves indicates clearly in his heavily Frazerian discussion of her sacred animals, who are she in beast disguise. Like Frazer, he explains myth as an extrapolation from natural history when he links the goddess with cat, wolf, and pig by virtue of their all feeding on corpse-flesh. Other qualities that intensify their foulness are the habits of mating openly and eating their own young.[34] Clearly the layer-out as the human version of the death-goddess would have to be equally repugnant in appearance and behavior. Like Yeats's black pig and Joyce's "cold mad feary father," she is the emblem of the triumphant antagonist, of the power that survives our personal decease and indifferently prepares our corpse for its final dissolution.

It is true that Graves does work out a cyclical pattern and a series of forms for the White Goddess. It is equally true, however, that he is not generally inclined to give each stage or guise the same amount of attention. He lavishes most of his efforts, particularly in his poetry, on exploring the goddess as temptress-mistress-destroyer. It is in this form that he describes her, in what apparently is her quintessential appearance: "The Goddess is a lovely, slender woman with a hooked nose, deathly pale face, lips red as rowan-berries, startlingly blue eyes and long fair hair." [35] All her other forms are but metamorphic versions of this archetypal image and so subordinate to it, for above all she is "the ancient power of fright and lust—the female spider or the queen-bee whose embrace is death." Why he should have focused on this image as central rather than that of the benevolent mother Demeter, or the dutiful wife Isis, or the serene virgin whether Persephone or Mary is uncertain. There may be personal reasons

34. The White Goddess, p. 235.
35. Ibid., p. 12.

or it may be more simply because she is the earliest form in which the image of woman captured his imagination. As early as 1922 he was responding to Keats's "La Belle Dame Sans Merci" in substantially the same fashion as he does in Chapter 24 of *The White Goddess,* some of which is composed of the last chapter from *The Meaning of Dreams* (1924).[36] It is clear at any rate that from virtually the beginning of his career Graves thought of love and poetry as related not so much through beauty as through their both being dangerous enterprises demanding daring and devotion in equal measures. When to this complex is added, as World War I and its nightmare-haunted aftermath did for Graves, death in all inexplicable horror, the nucleus of the Keatsian and Gravesian White Goddess is formed.

The notion of the beautiful woman who is whimsical, capricious, cruel, and tyrannical, and nonetheless passionately desired and sought after has a long literary tradition of which the medieval court of love portion is perhaps the best known. For such a figure the poet need not look beyond poetry or personal experience, but in Graves's case it is clear, from her name alone, that he has. His analogical imaginative habit impels him to link things that seem similar, whether they are literary, natural, or human in character. So, sharing in the early Keatsian vision of La Belle Dame and perhaps giving Graves a clue to understanding the most haunting of poems is *The Golden Bough*'s accounts of the great orgiastic fertility goddesses. Virtually all of these emphasize the awesome honor and responsibility of cohabiting with the divine woman. A number also stress the fertile mother aspect, but this belongs to that stage of the goddess following the one we are presently considering. By far the most pertinent treatment of her as the imperious sexual ruler of man is that provided by the discussion of the legend of Semiramis, queen of Assyria. Here Frazer describes a woman whose beauty won her the honor of becoming the king's wife even though she was a courtesan. Then, according to Frazer's account, "she won the

---

36. *On English Poetry,* p. 51. Graves, *The Common Asphodel* (London: Hamish Hamilton, 1949), p. vii; cf. *Poetic Unreason,* p. 62.

king's heart so far that she persuaded him to yield up to her the
kingdom for five days, and having assumed the sceptre and the
royal robes she made a great banquet on the first day, but on
the second day she shut up her husband in prison or put him
to death and thenceforward reigned alone." [37] Thereafter, to
avoid sharing her political power with a husband, she remained
single. But since chastity was not her metier, she "admitted to
her bed the handsomest of her soldiers, only, however, to destroy
them all afterwards." [38] This was done by burying them alive.

Such a creature has all the identifying characteristics of the
White Goddess as ruthless monarch of men. What makes her
even more clearly a central shaping force in Graves's image is the
fact that Frazer suggests that she is both an embodiment of the
Babylonian goddess of love and fertility Ishtar or Astarte and
also "a real queen of Assyria." To fuse in herself both the
archetypal dimensions of myth and the ceaseless variety of
quotidian reality, to be both goddess and flesh-and-blood woman
—when coupled with the aforementioned traits—is to provide
Graves with a model for his own multinamed goddess and
beloved. In addition to the evidence of the poems, which will be
discussed later, there is a final indication of the closeness of the
relationship between anthropologist and poet. Frazer links
Semiramis and her lovers with the Babylonian epic of Gilgamesh,
who avoids the fatal embraces of Ishtar whom Frazer in an
adumbration of Graves calls "the cruel goddess." In *The White
Goddess* Graves too identifies her as the betrayer of Gilgamesh
and likens her to Blodeuwedd in the *Mabinogian*, Delilah in the
Bible, and Deianira in classical myth, all of whom are regarded
as the third or love-goddess aspect of the pentad of roles played
by the White Goddess. [39]

Gilgamesh is, as Graves suggests and Frazer implies, a later
version of Tammuz, the original Babylonian lover of Ishtar, who
died and was reborn annually. The chief difference between them

37. *Golden Bough*, 9:369.
38. Ibid., 9:371.
39. *The White Goddess*, pp. 146, 343-44.

is that Gilgamesh rejects the love of the goddess while Tammuz reciprocates it. In the myth of the White Goddess as Graves elaborates it, the latter is correct. To avoid the goddess in order to remain safe, to retain tranquility and life, is to be guilty of masculine self-sufficiency. Out of this stems the passion for rational logic and patriarchal social institutions both of which serve to all but obliterate the goddess as a figure of public veneration. Graves does not devote any significant amount of attention to mythological versions of such evasions in *The White Goddess*. He does, however, have a good deal to say about the dereliction of manly duty practiced by what he calls classical poets (poets of all eras who follow reason and Apollo rather than passion and the White Goddess) and most of the modern age. The theme—the importance of submission to the goddess and her ritual of the seasons and life—is clearly central to Graves's mythopoeic pattern. But for its clearest and most significant cultural (as opposed to personal) delineation we must turn from *The White Goddess* to its dialectical counterpart, *King Jesus*.

## III

This novel was published two years after *Hercules, My Shipmate* and two before *The White Goddess*, which places it right at the heart of Graves's burgeoning myth. The crux of the novel is the historical role Graves adduces for Jesus together with the intellectual and cultural climate in which he places his tragic hero. Jesus is said to be the son of Miriam or Mary, the daughter of Joachim and Hannah, and Antipater, the son of Herod King of Israel. By marriage with Miriam, Antipater acquired a true title to rule in Israel which even his father Herod did not possess. According to his father's will, the succession to the throne was to move from Antipater to Herod Philip and then back to Antipater's heirs. With the death of Herod, the execution of Antipater, the abdication of Herod Philip, and the murder of Antipater the Younger, Antipater's other son, Jesus, is left possessing the right of succession. That this is both resolutely opposed in the novel and unrecorded in scriptural or other documents is explained as due to Antipater's marriage being a secret one. The central dramatic line of the novel, then, is Jesus' attainment of the secret of his birthright and his attempt to claim the spiritual power attendant upon it while rejecting the temporal.

His clash with the White Goddess and many of the reasons for it can be gleaned from the following passage which represents the opinions of the narrator, Agabus, an Alexandrian scholar purporting to write around A.D. 90.[40]

> As a sacred King, the last legitimate ruler of an immensely ancient dynasty, his avowed intention was to fulfil all the ancient prophecies that concerned himself and bring the history of his House to a real and unexceptionable conclusion. He intended by an immense exercise of power and perfect trust in God the Father to annul the boastful tradition of royal pomp—dependent on armies, battles, taxes, mercantile adventures, marriages with foreign princesses, Court luxury and popular oppression—which King Solomon had initiated at Jerusalem; and at the same time to break the lamentable cycle of birth, procreation, death and rebirth in which both he and his subjects had been involved since Adam's day. Merely to resign his claim to temporal power was not enough. His resolute hope was to defeat Death itself by enduring with his people the so-called Pangs of the Messiah, the cataclysmic events which were the expected prelude to the coming of the Kingdom of God; and his justification of this hope was the prophecy in the twenty-fifth chapter of Isaiah: "He shall destroy Death forever." In the Kingdom, which would be miraculously fertile and perfectly pacific, all Israelites would be his subjects who acknowledged him in his threefold capacity as king, prophet and healer, and under his benignant rule would live wholly free from error, want, sickness or fear of death for no less than a thousand years.[41]

40. The narrator claims on the first page, *King Jesus*, p. 7, to be writing his study from A.D. 89-93. In *The Nazarene Gospel Restored* (London: Cassell, 1953), p. xii n, Graves says he was writing in A.D. 98, which suggests a Faulknerian attitude toward consistency.

41. *King Jesus*, pp. 239-40.

One of the more important ways in which he contradicts the goddess's ritual is ignoring the fact that as a sacred king, he was her consort and subject to her authority. Breaking the cycle of birth-death-rebirth was the grossest violation of the stations of her year and of the pattern of existence she represented. To destroy Death was to annihilate the ultimate phase of her cycle. Similarly, his denial of "royal pomp," of material factors external to the individual human soul, is in essence a denial of the natural world itself on which the worship of the goddess is grounded. And finally, by assuming a threefold capacity capable of producing a paradisiacal and virtually immortal existence for his subjects, he is clearly parodying the trinity of her functions and the cyclic nature of her reign.

The most flagrant contradiction of her rule, however, comes with Jesus' enjoining chastity on all Israel as the price for destroying Death and entry into the Kingdom of God. As his wife Mary, the daughter of Cleopas, is told:

> Desire for progeny in marriage is an ancient error implanted in men and women by God's Adversary. . . . He has persuaded them that by this means they are staving off the ultimate victory of Death over mankind. . . . But the truth is that by performing the act of death they are yielding Death the victory.[42]

In assuming that this course of sexual abstinence is generally possible for and desirable to the faithful of Israel, Jesus is guilty either of confusing a spiritual with a temporal reality or of trying to hasten a state for which the moment had not yet come. The former seems to be Graves's own view as expressed through the texture and tone of the novel, while the latter is suggested by one of the characters, Mary the Hairdresser, who represents the goddess as the crone.

It is Jesus' confrontation with this Mary Magdalene at the Terebinth Fair which renders the clash between sacred king and

42. Ibid., p. 260.

fertility goddess, male and female religious principles, in its most dramatic and imagistic form. They engage in a ritual combat by way of offering rival and contradictory interpretations of the pictures on two tablets. These pictures render, Mary says, "the story of the ancient covenant from which the Ark takes its name; the covenant sworn between my Mistress and the twin Kings of Hebron; that she will share her love and her anger equally between them both so long as they obey her will." [43] Their struggle to assert the superiority of their respective deities culminates in a victory of the moment for Jesus when he expels the evil spirits from her and leads her out into the starlight and the land of life. Yet even at the moment of his apparent triumph there are forebodings that the goddess is not so easily thwarted. For one thing, Mary recites a prophetic poem which picking up their earlier identification with Adam and Eve also associates Adam-Jesus with Frazer's Hanged God, the sacrificial victim. And for another, even after she is divested of the evil spirits, her final words to Jesus are to the effect that "the end is not yet, and when the Mother summons me to my duty, I will not fail her." [44]

In delineating the character and origins of latter-day Christianity's regimen of ascetic chastity, Graves is not reflecting views or attitudes explicit in *The Golden Bough*. He may, however, be adapting its habit of showing the falsity of currently received views about the nature of Christ and Christianity. Frazer explodes the idea of the historical purity of Christianity by showing how much it derives from pagan religions that center on a dying and reviving god. In his discussion of the crucifixion of Christ he also provides Graves with a model for reinterpreting the event in terms that square with known rituals as well as with the demands for historical and documentary consistency. The reasons for Jesus' crucifixion adduced by Frazer and Graves are startlingly at odds with the traditional view; they are centered in rituals observed for the dying and reviving god of still earlier

43.  Ibid., p. 213.
44.  Ibid., p. 220.

times. Frazer suggests Jesus was cast in the role of Haman in the Jewish festival of Purim, which in turn derived from the Babylonian festival of the Sacaea, both of which were Saturnalia involving a mock king and his ritual death.[45] Graves does substantially the same thing, though he compounds the irony by stressing the orthodoxy of Jesus' Jewry while underscoring that his death takes the form of a ritual sacrifice to the heathen goddess he had opposed.

What makes *King Jesus* a reflection of the impact of *The Golden Bough* is not simply its hero's role as sacrificial scapegoat but the extent to which the cultural ambience in which he moves is suffused by the belief, customs, and images of the great fertility goddess. The impression created by the novel is that of the ancient Hebrew world being seen beneath a palimpset composed of patterns elaborated in *The Golden Bough.* Frazer's concern is largely with the Mediterranean religious world, and when he deals with its Semitic extensions, it is from a distance and with a certain measure of simplicity. Graves, on the other hand, gives us through names, genealogies, idiom, and customs a sense of the distinctively Hebraic caste of his world in much the same way as Thomas Mann does in *Joseph and His Brothers.* But to this he adds also a lively and vigorous impression of the extent to which this world was a part of the whole Mediterranean complex. He lets us see, in effect, Judaism growing out of earlier primitive religions and then standing at the verge of the origin of Christianity. And what one is impressed by is precisely what strikes one in *The Golden Bough,* the ways and the extent to which these religions have common grounds, however altered their symbols and displaced their rituals.

In the opening pages of *King Jesus* Graves quickly establishes the preeminence of the female deity as the hero's antagonist in several ways. The narrator, who has the same cool detached tone of the outsider as Frazer, reports that the Jews believed "they never owed any duty either to the Great Triple Moon-Goddess who is generally reputed to have mothered the Mediterranean races, or to any other goddess or nymph whatsoever." But then

45. *Golden Bough,* 9:355, 362-65, 412-23.

he proceeds to claim that their own sacred stories of their heroes disprove this belief.[46] Another and perhaps the most prominent way Graves emphasizes her importance is by the sheer proliferation of references to her worship, its customs, emblems, and forms. Elements of this order appearing at the outset and reminding us strongly of *The Golden Bough*'s stress are such things as premarital prostitution as a religious rite, self-castration on the same ground, ritual fornication to ensure flourishing crops, the rule of kings based on matrilineal succession and ultimogeniture, and the reddening of the god's face.[47] These references continue throughout the book and by so doing achieve several ends.

One is the saturating of the novel's background in the myths of the fertility goddess enunciated in *The White Goddess*. At the same time it adds highly detailed, concrete scenes of specific human beings who either believe in her and her powers or else whose minds and habits of behavior are saturated by the residue of her earlier position in Israel. As a result, the novel, unlike the equivalent essay or critical study, gives us a clear sense of the dynamics of the goddess's religion and worship. Instead of unfamiliar mythical figures like Blodeuwedd or Cerridwen we encounter a talking, breathing woman named Mary the Hairdresser (Magdala), whose appearance of "a tall blue-eyed hag, her nose crooked like a falcon's beak" reveals the goddess as crone.[48] From such details multiplied many times we see that for Graves history is a record, often confused and distorted, of life lived mythically and ritualistically. Therefore, the historical novel is an accurate imaginative re-creation of that life, a re-creation that both records and interprets by the use of what he calls the analeptic method.

To grasp the wide-ranging and intricate relationships and meanings provided by the mythic details that are both dramatized and analyzed in the novel is to see another goal they achieve. The concentration on the mother goddess and the extent to

46. *King Jesus*, p. 8.
47. Ibid., pp. 10, 20, 51, 67.
48. Ibid., p. 212.

which her religion underlies that of Israel in Jesus' day bears in on the reader that the whole career of Jesus and virtually the entire dramatic action of the novel conforms to the ritual pattern of the sacred king, her consort. Central to this pattern is the fact that, according to Graves, "in every country around the Mediterranean Sea, crucifixion was a fate reserved for the annual Sacred King" who was always "regarded as a sacrifice made on behalf of the tribe to its Goddess Mother." [49]

This directly entails the third end achieved by the novel's extensive reliance on mythic detail. For the ultimate point of the material is ironic, as Graves makes quite explicit. Jesus' rejection of the goddess is symbolized intellectually by his battle of wits with the hag and emotionally by his sexual abstention with his bride. Both women significantly have the same name, as does his mother. Nevertheless he is ultimately subjected to her power of death and resurrection and to playing the role in which he was cast by birth. To this irony of event Graves adds another by the tone with which he invests Jesus' story. Instead of the traditional tragic caste, he gives it an ironic perspective through his narrator. Agabus writes religious history with as strong a comparative bent as Frazer himself and with as keen an eye as that master ironist for the incongruities between human aspirations and achievements, beliefs and realities. Graves makes Jesus not only Frazer's dying and reviving god who ritualistically sacrifices himself that his people may be redeemed from a world of death, but also the sacred king who is the consort and ritual victim of the White Goddess. In effect, the irony is achieved by making the hero a myth within a myth, of which the ritual actions are identical in form and antithetical in purpose. The function of such irony, of course, is to validate dramatically the thesis enunciated in *The White Goddess*, namely, that she can be flouted only at the individual's peril because her ritual embodies the fundamental and ineluctable course of life itself.

49. Ibid., pp. 338-39. The whole discussion here of this custom is heavily indebted to *The Golden Bough* as its comparative manner, its reference to yearly surrogates (in a historical sequence of son, prisoner, and criminal), and the use of myth as explanation and warrant for ritual attest.

# CHAPTER III

# The White Goddess and the Beloved Victim

On the basis of the controlling themes in *The White Goddess* and *King Jesus* it might appear that a myth of this sort would prove constrictive to the artist using it exhaustively and assiduously as Graves does. Whether such is the case can best be seen from his poems, which, he says, represent the significant and dedicated portion of his career. The goddess and her human victim do figure prominently in a number of them. Yet there are also a great many poems that explore other facets of the universe he has derived from *The Golden Bough*. The important poetic motifs fall under three main headings. The first includes all those poems that treat of the natural world as fact and emblem. The second group consists of poems dealing with spirits, nightmare, ghosts, magical spells, and the like. These coalesce into a vision of what might be called the other world in which the twin foci are demon and dream. The final motif to be distinguished is, broadly, that of the human world. There man performs numerous unsuspected rites of devotion that express his recognition of the divine, preternatural character investing all modes of life. These are poems that render the many faces and moods of the goddess and her human victim as well as ones that dramatize their own versions of phallic myths and classical legends.

While the majority of these poems are dramatic lyrics, a substantial number of others are satiric in tone. As such, they perform an important function. They shear away the layers of uncritical respect and devotion that surround many of the myths Graves deals with. They also make clear that the present is as vulnerable to the irony of time, circumstance, and personality as the past. In this way Graves avoids making his myth of the White Goddess appear a product of pseudoreligiosity or of occult wish fulfillment. Actually it is an extended metaphor for the vicissitudes and exaltation that come to man both from the external world of nature and mankind and from the internal world of his own metabolism and psyche. And in large measure what Graves provides is a test of his readers' capacity to distinguish between poetic and prosaic methods of thought. The former he describes as the ability "to resolve speech into its original images and rhythms and re-combine these on several simultaneous levels of thought into a multiple sense." [1] In a sense, this is the central connection between *The White Goddess* and the poems: the prose of the former is transformed into the poetry of the latter and to understand both a capacity to apprehend metaphor is essential.

Of the three motifs, clearly that of the human world whose paradigm is the White Goddess and her sacred king-victim is the most important. Nevertheless, the others are also significant, for they provide a background that serves as a symbolic reflector of the central myth. In addition, they create irradiating circles of image and statement which permit the metaphor of myth the necessary scope in which to reveal its real nature as the ordering force of imagination. But to see this most clearly one needs a distinct picture of the goddess motif and its development.

Poems presenting the goddess may be divided into those which name or otherwise explicitly identify her and those which do not but instead seem ostensibly concerned with purely human subjects. The latter afford us the chance to see both the growth of this figure and also the manner in which she merges into the human so that goddess and woman become extensions of one another. Early instances of this are found in "The Hills of May" and "Love in Barrenness." Both use the image of the wind as a woman's lover to show the poignancy and exaltation of love.

"The Hills of May" has the wind narrate the course of the

1. *The White Goddess*, p. 236.

love from intimacy of a natural, spiritual order through indifference to human contact to a lament for the departure of the nameless and incomparable female. It is in just this pattern of easy action, unrestrained enjoyment, and casual departure that the lineaments of the White Goddess can be seen, even though at the time of writing Graves had no such concept clearly formulated. Also contributing to the sense of her presence is the opening description of her "Walking with a virgin heart / The green hills of May"; the reference to "her untied hair"; and her proud behavior, which reaches its apex in "So she loved with a whole heart, / Neglecting man." Though the diction is predominantly Georgian and much concerned with rural England in a nebulous but distant past, still, all these elements produce a pattern very like that which Graves built up with the assistance of *The Golden Bough*. The chief difference lies in the tone affected. This early poem, while prepared to celebrate the superiority of the female, does so in the false accents of Victorian idealizing and early Yeatsian aestheticism: "She has left our bournes for ever, / Too fine to stay."

In this respect, "Love in Barrenness" is an improvement, for it points up the sexual role played by the image of the wind as lover and concludes on the typically Gravesian note of the irresistibility of the beloved's beauty:

> The North Wind rose: I saw him press
> With lusty force against your dress,
> Moulding your body's inward grace
> And streaming off from your set face;
> So now no longer flesh and blood
> But poised in marble flight you stood.
> O wingless Victory, loved of men,
> Who could withstand your beauty then?

Lurking just back of or pointing toward the image of the wind as lover is the anthropological commonplace discussed by Frazer that certain peoples are ignorant of the causes of conception and so attribute it to various animals, plants, ghosts, and spirits. The function of the image here, however, is not to point toward a primitive or mythic orientation for the poem. Rather it is to convey the metamorphic power of desire and the intimate parallels between nature and man. Together they form and create a single universe, that of art, in which the real power of man is the capacity of accepting his vanquishment by beauty.

In these poems the beloved is not identified, except when she has been transformed into her sculptural analogue. But in "The Last Day of Leave" Graves partially rectifies that omission in the course of a reflective contemplation of the past and the varieties of love shared by him and his friends. While all the others are in love with specific persons, he is "As deep in love with a yet nameless muse." In context the remark is casual but nevertheless very significant, for it indicates an early, almost intuitive iden-tification of poetry and the beloved. In addition, the poem's use of the past tense and "yet" suggests that by the time of writing the muse had been more clearly identified, though still not given her final title of the White Goddess.

Clarifying the precise relationship obtaining between muse and devotee is the poem "Gardener" which uses the image of a gardener, who though clumsy nevertheless produces exceptional flowers and fruit, to body forth the mysteries of artistic creation. His secret and the world's response to it is set forth in the middle stanza:

> Yet none could think it simple awkwardness;
> And when he stammered of a garden-guardian,
> Said the smooth lawns came by angelic favour,
> The pinks and pears in spite of his own blunders,
> They nudged at this conceit.

Here in substance is Graves's own basic response to his poetic art and the divine force that makes it possible. The White Goddess, both the concept and the book, is his own stammering effort to convey to the uninformed what compensates for his own personal inadequacies and brings his creative effort to fruition.

That Graves should focus his attention upon a figure in which strangeness and simple beauty are united is understandable when we look back at "The Ages of Oath." This poem muses on the child's possession of, and the adult's loss and regaining of, delight in "the especial sight." To the child, "The lost, the freakish, the unspelt / Drew me: for simple sights I had no eye." To the adult, it is the beloved who is unique and utterly different and so the object of his admiration. For the one, it is the natural and unusual objects, such as "a garden-tulip growing / Among wild primroses of a wild field, / Or a cuckoo's egg in a black-bird's nest," that delight and captivate. For the other, it is the human subject, the woman capable of reducing him to "stammering out my praise of you, / Like a boy owning his first love," that enthralls and gives him the capacity "to know deeply." This juxtaposition of natural and human which yet agrees on the value of the exceptional suggests its own ultimate unreality. Both are aspects, faces if you will, of the goddess whose history and metamorphoses are as bizarre as those discoveries of the child.

The centrality of strangeness to the goddess is nowhere better exhibited than in the short but powerful poem "On Portents":

> If strange things happen where she is,
> So that men say that graves open
> And the dead walk, or that futurity
> Becomes a womb and the unborn are shed,
> Such portents are not to be wondered at,
> Being tourbillions in Time made
> By the strong pulling of her bladed mind
> Through that ever-reluctant element.

Strangeness is not only her medium but also the result of her action on Time construed as the ground of change. That her signs should take the form of whirlwinds is but the converse of her taking the wind as her lover. Her presence is known by what happens to the empirically real, conventionally visible elements in the world. And the fundamental nature of that presence is defined by the last two lines, which stress both the indomitability of the goddess and the passive opposition of her antagonist. Time in its conventionality takes the form of a resistance to change or metamorphosis even when occurring in the cyclic pattern embodied in the goddess as nature deity. The phrase "the strong pulling of her bladed mind" also conveys in subtle naturalistic fashion the goddess's nature and response to those who oppose her. The blade of her mind and its action adumbrates the action of her double axe in beheading her consort when he has fulfilled his term of office.

While the poem does not make it clear, some comments on it in *The White Goddess* explain why Time is the adversary of the Muse. According to Graves, all original discoveries and artistic creations are "the result of proleptic thought—the anticipation, by means of a suspension of time, of a result that could not have been arrived at by inductive reasoning—and of what may be called analeptic thought, the recovery of lost events by the same suspension." [2] Since "in the poetic act, time is suspended," [3] the images in "On Portents" of the bladed mind and reluctant element accurately render the beheading of a personified convention which, Graves says, though useful has no intrinsic value.

## II

A full-blown and direct exploration of the goddess and what she means to man is undertaken in section 8 of the *Collected Poems* (1959) which begins with the dedicatory poem from *The White Goddess*. In its three stanzas the world's view of the goddess is defined, the poet's quest of her traced, her appearance recounted, and the response to her nature shown. Here one sees how completely Graves has managed to integrate what he learned from *The Golden Bough* into his own developing vision. The opening lines—"All saints revile her, and all sober men /

2. Ibid., p. 376.
3. Ibid., p. 377.

Ruled by the God Apollo's golden mean"—pick up *The Golden Bough*'s stress on the church's antipathy to pagan religions and add to it Graves's own aversion to the simple-minded rationalism of the prosaic. While Frazer's rationalism often seems to be of this sort, its thoroughgoing lack of dogmatism makes it a much more flexible instrument of thought than that of those Graves attacks. In any case, *The Golden Bough* by its concentration on the incredible metamorphoses of witches, the primitive confusion of dreams and reality, and the trances of medicine men and patients alike refutes in its subject matter the idea that sober rationalism encompasses all the meaningful experiences of mankind. And in the immediately succeeding lines Graves further reveals his affinities with Frazer. He uses the same image of a sea voyage to strange and distant regions in search of a religious secret as *The Golden Bough* employs at the end of its very first chapter. In both cases the voyage involves the extremes of geography and climate and the threatening possibilities of lost direction. In so doing it provides an image that symbolically sums up the scope and dangers of the comparative method that underlies the achievement of both men.

When we come to the goddess herself, there is less resemblance to the great female fertility deities described by Frazer. Here Graves stresses largely her attractiveness and only lightly suggests her associations with death and disfigurement:

> Whose broad high brow was white as any leper's,
> Whose eyes were blue, with rowan-berry lips,
> With hair curled honey-coloured to white hips.

It is, however, in the note of foreboding struck by the leper reference that the possible influence of Frazer appears. He discusses the Mexican customs of worshipping a goddess of lepers named Atlatonan and of sacrificing lepers to the maiden maize goddess.[4] The maize goddess, though younger than

---

4. *Golden Bough*, 7:261; 9:291-92. The chief difference is that the White Goddess, unlike the Mexican deities, is never sacrificed for fertility or any other reasons.

Graves's description suggests, is described as having long hair and wearing various decorations and ornaments that were golden in color. We have already seen Graves's associating the pig with the White Goddess as her sacred animal in a manner derived from *The Golden Bough*. Since Frazer also suggests that leprosy results either from drinking pig's milk or injuring a sacred totemic animal, it is easy to see how Graves links the disease with the goddess.[5] Her whiteness serves as a warning of her immense power that is capable of inflicting such a dread disease. It also is a prophecy of the inescapable and steady dissolution of all who are subject to her sway. But as a complexion shade, it is regarded as particularly desirable and attractive. Therefore, it also reminds us that she is a woman and that the beautiful and the ugly, the desirable and the revolting, the good and the evil, may subsist together. Like Moby Dick she points up the relativity of symbols and their amenability to metamorphosis and modulation, themes which emerge powerfully in *The Golden Bough*.

Finally, in the last stanza, the poem exhibits the attitude proper to the questers and all worshippers of the White Goddess and distinguishes it from that of the rest of the world:

> Green sap of Spring in the young wood a-stir
> Will celebrate the Mountain Mother,
> And every song-bird shout awhile for her;
> But we are gifted, even in November
> Rawest of seasons, with so huge a sense
> Of her nakedly worn magnificence
> We forget cruelty and past betrayal,
> Heedless of where the next bright bolt may fall.

Animal and vegetable life extol the goddess as their creative source but only in season or according to their abilities. The human being, however, who is gifted with consciousness and will, as symbolized in his quest, alone is capable of the ultimate response to the goddess. Confronted with the wholly open,

5. Ibid., 8:24-26.

unconcealed beauty of reality which is truth, the human quester finds it reward enough. The stages of sacrifice and death that inevitably follow such an initiation are accepted almost unwittingly or indifferently as well worth the price.[6] Such a pursuit of truth at the cost of life itself resembles that of Frazer whose devotion to this ideal has been pointed out in an earlier chapter. And indeed, it may well have been *The Golden Bough* and its author who reinforced Graves's feeling that truth is a divine attribute and one worth worshipping.

Of the other poems in this section of the *Collected Poems* those immediately following "The White Goddess" are largely rearrangements and translations of poems dealt with in *The White Goddess*. As such they fall somewhat outside of our main concern, though not wholly because Graves's revisions are so far-reaching that they virtually constitute new poems. And insofar as they are the product of his imagination in large measure they too may be read for traces of *The Golden Bough* as a shaping force. It is perhaps significant that the three poems of Celtic origin all develop various aspects of the theme of creation, order, and identity. By so doing they provide a clear contrast with a later group in the section that deals with death and the inevitable loss of the goddess's company.

Because of their early Celtic origin specific instances of Frazer's impact are less clearly visible than in those poems authored solely by Graves. Nevertheless, there are some elements that *The Golden Bough* may have helped to accentuate. Thus, in "The Song of Blodeuwedd" Graves stresses the magical character of the creation or birth of the May-queen goddess, the intricate vegetative nature bestowed on her, and the magical significance of the number *nine*. Each of these elements receives substantial treatment in general terms in *The Golden Bough*.[7] That is to say, Frazer does not deal directly with the poem or with Celtic mythology, but ·he does point up the marvelous births experienced by many gods, many of which involve vegeta-

---

6. The identification of the goddess with Truth poetically apprehended, though not overt here, is made explicit in *The White Goddess*, p. 502.

7. *Golden Bough*, 2:59-96, 97-101; 1:109; 3:302-4, 307; 9:8; 10:235.

tion as in the case of Adonis and Attis. Similarly, his stress on the symbolic association of various plants with various deities may have contributed substantially to Graves's reconstruction of the poem which makes the goddess a composite vegetative deity:

> Nine powers in me combined,
> Nine buds of plant and tree.

Here the impact of *The Golden Bough* would be primarily methodological thought arrived at through its subject matter. Doubtless much learning of other sorts and from other sources have gone into Graves's researches on the White Goddess. One can still, however, detect Frazer's contribution in the provision of those items which would leap out from the confused mass of material that is the original Celtic poem. In short, Graves was clearly choosing the lines to be included in this poem according to some rationale, and, however subterranean or unconscious it was, it seems likely that Frazer contributed something to it.

Similarly, in "Amergin's Charm" Graves expands the original and in so doing shows himself receptive to some of the images and symbolic patterns developed in *The Golden Bough*. Lines are added and others are altered, usually by expansion. Thus, in the original translation Graves uses as his point of departure for revisions, a line reads "I am a boar" with an accompanying gloss that says "for valour." In Graves this becomes "I am a boar: *renowned and red*," which clearly seeks to introduce the image of the goddess's consort who suffers a fatal wound by the boar, who gains a kind of fame as the enemy of the god. The elaborate attention paid this myth by Frazer in the *Adonis, Attis, Osiris* volumes needs no emphasizing. Similarly, the color *red* is employed perhaps as natural history and as the death color of primitive times. The latter notion, advanced in *The White Goddess*, Graves may very well have derived from Frazer who records its use in connection with manslayers, sacrifices, and adornment of the gods.[8] The iconography of *The Golden Bough* in the hands of an imaginative and speculatively daring writer

8.  Ibid., 2:175 ff.; 3:175, 179, 185; 6:97, 106; 7:260, 261, 263; 8:34; 9:213.

like Graves yields a line which in compressed fashion renders the slaying of the handsome young man, who is the goddess's consort, by his antagonist. The latter is both a murderer and a ritual sacrificer acting in accord with the dictates of the season and also the god who is to supplant the consort until his own term of office shall have expired.

In much the same way, the immediately following lines are transmuted so as to emphasize the seasonal and human end of life:

> I am a breaker: *threatening doom,*
> I am a tide: *that drags to death.*

Though his commentary in *The White Goddess* on these lines focuses on the Irish context, it would be surprising if he did not also mean to suggest the movement of the prehistoric thirteen-month year through its cycle in a number of contexts. Both lines suggest the myths recounting the deaths of Hippolytus and Adonis as described by Frazer. It was the roar of the sea, acting in accordance with Poseidon's command, that frightened Hippolytus's horses and caused him to be *dragged* to his death. And, less clearly connected, in the rituals at the death of Adonis images of him are set afloat and sent out to perish amid the waves of the sea.

Similarly, the final lines are not simply a Gravesian dramatization of the five stations of the goddess as well as of the vowels of an ancient Celtic alphabet. They also derive their controlling form from *The Golden Bough* with its myths of birth, fruition, and death in which human and vegetative forms are subtly intertwined so that they serve as seasonal mirrors of one another. Thus, insofar as the poem is a celebration of godhead in its multiform appearances, it takes its creative cue from Frazer in that it sees the importance for mankind of vegetative fertility: "I am the womb: *of every holt.*" The next stage, that of initiation, identifies the deity with "the blaze: *on every hill,*" strongly recalling *The Golden Bough*'s discussion of fire as a purificatory element and a sacred and hence protective force, especially in the midsummer festivals. Since the last two lines seem to owe no specific debt to Frazer, the final sign of his impact comes in "I am the queen: *of every hive."* The image of the queen bee for the goddess, the divine woman, is a popular one with Graves, largely one gathers because of her renowned ruthless use and disposition of her male cohorts. At the same time, it is unlikely that anyone so interested in comparative mythology and so familiar with *The Golden Bough* would have forgotten Frazer's account of the Ephesian Artemis, one of whose emblems is numerous bees and whose worship involved several men serving the goddess in complete chastity for a year, an office which carried with it the title of King Bee.[9]

"The Battle of the Trees," even in Graves's version, does not seem to show any unmistakable signs of Frazer's influence. This is largely because there is less departure from the original translation than in the other poems. In relation to the poems of this section, it does, however, have a structural significance derived from the ritual patterns recounted in *The Golden Bough* and codified by later writers such as Gilbert Murray and S. H. Hooke. According to *The White Goddess,* this poem recounts a struggle for supremacy between two peoples in ancient Ireland in which the winner replaces the loser's deity with his own. The outcome of the struggle is contingent upon guessing the secret name of the opposing deity, a contest that marks it as a form of ritual combat, which Murray identifies as the first of the ritual forms detectable in Greek tragedy. Since the preceding poems in the section have concentrated on birth and creation as expressions of the godhead, "The Battle of the Trees" clearly is the next phase of life, the struggle for survival, the combat in which either the god or his antagonist must suffer defeat and death.

The legitimacy of this view is supported by the poem which follows it. Like the others, it too is a translation or free adaptation from an early source, in this case, certain Orphic tablets found in Roman and Cretan tombs that aim to provide the occupants

9. Ibid., 1:37; 2:135-36.

with, as Jane Harrison says, "instructions for his conduct in the world below, exhortations to the soul, formularies to be repeated, confessions of faith and of ritual performed, and the like." [10] Indeed, Graves calls it "Instructions to the Orphic Adept" and like Harrison he makes his version of the tablet a description of the appropriate ritual behavior for someone who is entering the underworld of death and darkness. The keynote of this behavior is memory, which is contrasted with the sterility and vulgarity of forgetfulness:

> So soon as ever your mazed spirit descends
> From daylight into darkness, Man, remember
> What you have suffered here in Samothrace,
> What you have suffered.

The elements added by Graves are those of the "mazed spirit" and Samothrace. The first of these immediately suggests a poeticism describing the dazed surprise of the individual who has just experienced the critical rite of death and its attendant transformation of light into darkness. But read in the light of the sixth chapter of *The White Goddess*, entitled "A Visit to Spiral Castle," as well as the works of Frazer and Jane Harrison, the phrase takes on more elaborately traditional and mythic significance. The germane topics treated in this chapter are Orpheus and his relation to other heroes, the burial grounds of Irish and other sacred kings, and myths and rituals connected with the labyrinth. They combine to suggest unmistakably that the spirit addressed is that of a Theseus-like hero who finding himself in a labyrinth or maze will push on to his goal. This involves a confrontation with nescience over which he will triumph by choosing the consciousness of memory, which, as Graves observes, involves the future as well as the past. Such a conquest is a triumph over death and a return to fertility and life. As Graves suggests, the maze pattern is twofold, carrying one

10. Harrison, *Prolegomena to the Study of Greek Religion* (New York: Meridian, 1955), p. 572. Her chapter on "Orphic Eschatology" together with the Critical Appendix on the tablets by Gilbert Murray are unquestionably Graves's sources for this poem.

into the very center of the mysterious threat to life and then winding back out to safety. Insofar as man is a follower of Orpheus, he must face the fact of his mortality and continue to live without forgetting or denying that fact.

If the hero is Orpheus, at least on one level, then the memory of what he has suffered would obviously be his savage dismemberment at the hands of the Thracian maenads. But Graves is quite explicit in his reference to Samothrace, and so far as the various forms of his myth reveal, Orpheus did not meet his death there. A partial explanation of this can be found in Jane Harrison and Frazer. The former suggests that Samothrace was "the natural bridge between Orientalized Asia Minor and the mainland" by means of which the Orphic stress on elemental deities like earth and sky entered Greece to oppose the arid rationalism and formalism of the Olympians.[11] At the same time, Frazer describes the Samothracian mysteries as involving a dramatic representation of the marriage of Cadmus and Harmonia —a rite representing, he says, the mythical marriage of the sun and moon. The implications of these points are that the hero experienced a sacred marriage with the moon-goddess on the island of Samothrace. This, in turn, identifies him as the sacred king, the consort of the White Goddess, who, according to Graves, is buried "on an island, either in the river or the sea, where his spirit lived under charge of oracular and orgiastic priestesses."[12]

From this, the appropriateness of Samothrace to the action of the poem is clear. At the same time, the conjunction of the Orphic and Cadmean myths illuminates the injunction to remember addressed to the hero. It again suggests the subtle interrelations obtaining between marriage and death as rituals involving a crisis of transition. It also balances the experience of death against that of marriage so that, ideally, the terror of one is offset by the ecstasy of the other. In both a ritual of consummation is enacted. And to remember the sacred marriage of Samothrace is both to

11. Harrison, *Themis* (New York: University Books, 1962), p. 464.
12. *The White Goddess*, p. 108.

understand why one is experiencing the labrynthine confrontation with death in Samothrace and to know that the latter is not
final but will in the course of time yield to victory and a new
marriage, a new union with the White Goddess.

The second stanza is both the longest and the one which
follows the Orphic tablets most closely. Consequently, there is
little to attribute to the influence of *The Golden Bough*, except
for the possible shaping effect it may have had on Graves's
choice of lines, phrases, and images from the incomplete variants
of the tablets. Thus, while they make no mention of the dead
person's trip to the underworld, Graves remarks on the passage
through "Hell's seven floods." Possibly this may owe something
to Frazer's treatment of cases in which seven figures, in rituals
designed to placate the dead, attain purification and so fertility,
and perform sacrifices.[13] In both instances, the stress is on what
Arnold van Gennep calls liminal rites, those acts of transition
which move literally or figuratively from one state to another.[14]
Similarly, Graves follows the tablets in placing a cypress tree
beside the pool or spring of forgetfulness and from his remarks
in *The White Goddess* it is clear he regards the tree as a symbol
of resurrection.[15] And while there is no better place for such a
symbol than a place of death, there is still the necessity of
preserving the complexity of scene established in the first stanza
whereby life must be regained from the midst of death. To
this end, Graves makes the spring of forgetfulness black,
presumably to recall the figure of the crone or death-goddess,
and describes Hades, which he calls "the Halls of Judgment,"
as "a miracle of jasper and onyx." In *The White Goddess* jasper
is linked with the second to the last month of the year and so with
winter and death.[16] Hence its use in the poem serves to remind
us that the symbol of resurrection flourishes in a place reserved
for death.

13. *Golden Bough*, 2:32; 10:213; 4:74 ff.
14. Van Gennep, *The Rites of Passage*, tr. M. B. Vizadom and G. L. Caffee (London:
Routledge & Kegan Paul, 1960), p. 11.
15. *The White Goddess*, p. 285.
16. Ibid., pp. 221, 290, 292.

The next stanza is almost completely original with Graves save only the mention of the pool of memory and its guardians:

> To the right hand there lies a secret pool
> Alive with speckled trout and fish of gold;
> A hazel overshadows it, Ophion,
> Primaeval serpent straggling in the branches,
> Darts out his tongue. This holy pool is fed
> By dripping water; guardians stand before it.
> Run to this pool, the pool of Memory,
> Run to this pool!

In populating the pool of memory with speckled trout and a hazel tree, he seems to be following Celtic legends about the wisdom associated with them and the powers of divination they confer, though for some inexplicable reason he substitutes trout for salmon. In any event, from his mention of these tales and of other evidence for the powers attributed to the hazel in *The White Goddess*, it is clear that he has borrowed much of his knowledge from *The Golden Bough*.

A more direct borrowing may perhaps be seen in the image of the "fish of gold." Frazer recounts a poem about a golden fish who hidden in a secret pool in a man's garden contains the external soul of his adopted daughter. The fish is associated with the girl's capacity for consciousness so that when it comes into the hands of the evil queen, the girl lapses into unconsciousness. This state is identical with that suffered by the Orphic initiate in the rites of Trophonius, which, Harrison suggests, underlie the accounts on the tablets. She is ultimately revived by the king at nightfall who restores the golden fish to its pool and then marries her.[17] This is not to say that Graves is using the golden fish as an allegorical emblem for this story. Rather, the story, involving as it does the themes of beauty, the loss and recovery of consciousness, and the hints of metempsychosis, explains the choice of the image and the kind of symbolic appropriateness it assumes for the author.

17. *Golden Bough*, 9:147-48.

Less private in its significance but of essentially the same order is the allusion to Ophion, who was consigned to the underworld by Eurynome for claiming to be the creator of the world.[18] The mythic reference reminds us of the supremacy of the goddess and of the swift punishment visited upon those who infringe on her powers and prerogatives. In so doing it harks back to the Samothracian suffering with which the poem opened. At the same time, it derives an additional point from Jane Harrison and Frazer. They emphasize that the serpent is the original form of the hero and god, that he is peculiarly intimate with Aesculapius, the healing god who restored the dead to life, and that Cadmus the dragonslayer becomes a serpent at the end of his life.[19] In addition, the serpent guardian of various sacred springs is described by Frazer as having "in its custody both the instruments of divination, the holy tree and the holy water." [20]

There can be little doubt that all of these notions, and perhaps more, were moving and working together in the mythically conscious mind of Graves. What they add up to in terms of the poem is a complex vision of the interrelation of the godlike hero and the demonic, of wisdom and subterranean experience, of resurrection and self-transformation. To gain the power of true divination and understanding symbolized by the hazel, the holy pool, and the serpent, one must confront the fact that immortality is possible only to those who remember, that is, to those for whom time is suspended. Yet rebirth is possible only after death, which in turn, as the serpent's sloughing off his skin suggests, need not be final. Thus, since the Orphics thought to escape the tedious round of existence with its progression through birth, death, and rebirth, the poem also follows the same course.

The hero confronts the guardians of the pool, declares his need, identifies himself as an Orphic and as "child of the three-

---

18. *The Greek Myths*, 1:28.

19. Harrison, *Prolegomena*, pp. 18-21, and chapter 7; *Golden Bough*, 4:84.

20. *Golden Bough*, 4:80.

fold Queen of Samothrace," and proclaims his completion of the purificatory ritual that takes him "Out of the weary wheel, the circling years, / To that still, spokeless wheel:—Persephone." The guardians reply with a summation of what happens to the man transformed into a god and become immortal: he becomes a ruler of the dead and an oracular echo speaking from his tomb. The accuracy of this rendering of primitive Greek thought, at least as delineated by Jane Harrison, and the poetic power with which Graves invests it cannot obscure the fact that for the modern mind this has a peculiarly ironic and satisfactory ring to it. To become a memory preeminent only among other memories, a voice whose only presence is architectural, is not to achieve a great deal when set against the religious ideals and aspirations man has created for himself from such early times. And yet in the final irony, Graves may be implying, this is all that man can hope to achieve—to be remembered for yet a little while.

## III

Mortality, then, is what Graves's poem initiates the reader into and confirms as inescapable. It creates a tension between its own implications and the statements of its subject, between Graves the earthy lover of life and Jane Harrison's Orphics, who ascetically elaborate a doctrine of renunciation through which they feel their desired release from the world. In the poems that immediately follow in this section, there is no such conflict between the author and his material. Freed from the limiting conditions imposed by the Orphic tablets, Graves humanizes his myths and rituals and in so doing gives them a greater measure of credibility. Perhaps the most poignant illustration of this process occurs in "Lament for Pasiphaë," the first of these poems. The underlying myth is the bizarre classical story of the queen who conceived a passion for the bull sent by the god, but the story is seen from the perspective of *The Golden Bough*. "The legend appears to reflect a mythical marriage of the sun and moon, which was acted as a solemn rite by the king and queen of Cnossus, wearing the masks of a bull and cow respectively." [21]

What Graves does is to focus on the human beings beneath the masks. Thus, the first stanza is cast in the accents of a person caught between human reluctance to lose love and recognition of the ineluctability of the rituals of nature:

> Dying sun, shine warm a little longer!
> My eye, dazzled with tears, shall dazzle yours,
> Conjuring you to shine and not to move.
> You, sun, and I all afternoon have laboured
> Beneath a dewless and oppressive cloud—
> A fleece now gilded with our common grief
> That this must be a night without a moon.
> Dying sun, shine warm a little longer!

As Frazer suggests, the astronomical "lovers enjoyed each other's company at the time when the luminaries are in conjunction, namely, in the interval between the old and the new moon. Hence on the principles of sympathetic magic that interval was considered the time most favorable for human marriages. When the sun and moon are wedded in the sky, men and women should be wedded on earth. And for the same reason the ancients chose the interlunar day for the celebration of the Sacred Marriages of gods and goddesses." [22]

Such an occasion would seem to call for joyous celebrations rather than the lament we meet with here, but that is only because we have not widened our anthropological context sufficiently. Indeed, nothing more clearly reveals the extent and importance of Graves's reliance on Frazer than this particular situation. The latter's account of Pasiphaë appears in the volume entitled *The Dying God* in the chapter called "The Killing of the Divine King." And the burden of his argument here is that ancient Greek kings held office only for a limited term, usually

21. Ibid., 4:71.
22. Ibid., p. 73.

eight years, at the end of which time he was either renewed in the position or forfeited it depending on whether or not any foreboding omens or portents were observed, such as aberrant astronomical movements or declining virility on the king's part. Frazer thus thinks it likely that "among the solemn ceremonies which marked the beginning or the end of the eight years' cycle the sacred marriage of the king with the queen played an important part." [23]

In the poem Graves is opting for the sacred marriage as a ritual marking the end of the cycle, as bringing the worshippers, king, queen, god, and goddess to a point of crisis It is not a celebration of a coronation but the beginning of a period which is a test and trial for all. The worshipper tearfully confronted with a "dying sun" and "a night without a moon" faces a world devoid of deities, which in the primitive world is a prospect of shattering dimensions. The king as Minos at the end of his reign must look forward to withdrawing for a season to an oracular cave where he must justify his reign to the supreme deity, the father, and by contact with the godhead renew those sacred powers that allow him to reign once more.[24] And the queen approaches the ritual marriage knowing the full weight of ambiguity in the phrase "dying sun." Should consummation not be achieved, the king her husband and the representative of the god upon whom the country is dependent for its fertility is doomed. On the other hand, should it be effected, the ritual of the White Goddess, of the Astarte-Semiramis figure who carries one not only into marriage but through it to death, must without regard for personal feeling grind on its preordained cycle of ecstasy and misery.

It is precisely this kind of dilemma which gives the poem much of its weight and density of emotion. Reinforcing the dilemma is the sense of an overwhelming desire to restrain or freeze time coupled with a clear premonition that this is impossible. To further emphasize this, Graves subtly introduces

23. Ibid., p. 71.
24. Ibid., p. 70.

a related symbolic complex. The labors of the speaker and sun and the metaphoric transformation of the cloud into a black fleece take on point when we understand that such black rams or sheep were involved in rain-making ceremonies with the divine king and also were sacrificed at funeral games as "the characteristic offerings to the dead." [25] Despite their efforts the cloud remains "dewless and oppressive" and the fleece is gilded not with the gold of the mythic savior from death, as in the case of Phrixos and Helle, but with the black of night, sorrow, and death.

The first stanza renders the central situation in dramatic terms that accentuate the conflict between love and duty, the human desire and the religious necessity. The second stanza functions more nearly as explanation and commentary, as etiological myth to the ritual of marriage and death in the first stanza. In so doing, it not only turns to the past, it also adds a fresh dimension to the human anguish and thereby reveals a new depth to the love whose end is being lamented here:

> Faithless she was not: she was very woman,
> Smiling with dire impartiality,
> Sovereign, with heart unmatched, adored of men,
> Until Spring's cuckoo with bedraggled plumes
> Tempted her pity and her truth betrayed.
> Then she who shone for all resigned her being,
> And this must be a night without a moon.
> Dying sun, shine warm a little longer!

Having concentrated on the sun and king in the first stanza, the narrator here turns to the moon and the queen, Pasiphaë herself, and in so doing modulates the tone from one of pity and regret for the sun-king to that of exculpation and reverent love for the maligned moon-queen. Pasiphaë was not, it is argued, guilty of either literal or metaphoric bestiality, of perversion or lust. She was herself, the quintessence of womanhood as defined by Graves, serenely meeting her needs without

---

25. Ibid., p. 104; see also 1:290; 3:154; cf. *The Greek Myths*, 2:222.

committing herself to more than the momentary. In this calm, generous, affectionate estimate one hears not only the voice of the devoted worshipper but that of Minos himself. Knowing her and loving her, he understands the integral sufficiency of the female and through this the inviolable and irremediable character of the individual nature and temperament.

Perhaps because this stanza does take on the sound of an understanding husband who grasps the dynamics of behavior and personality that have led his wife to cuckold him, we find the second half of it offering an extenuating explanation in terms of what might be called mythic history. Pasiphaë was "sovereign" and direly impartial until the appearance of the cuckoo of spring. This, however, is an allusion to the disguise by which Zeus was ultimately able to woo and seduce Hera, his twin sister.[26] As a result, it appears that Graves here is running remarkably close to Yeats's use of the Leda myth; both find the explanation to a cataclysmic event in an earlier historical event. Graves, however, differs in that he fuses two myths between which there is no independent causal connection. The reason for this is to provide an explanation for the moon-goddess's disappearance, one consonant with his frequently reiterated thesis—the disastrous effects of supplanting a matriarchy with a patriarchal society. In *The Greek Myths* he argues that Hera was the pre-Hellenic Great Goddess and that her forced marriage to Zeus is a mythic rendering of political conquests of territories that worshipped her, conquests that spelled the end of her religious supremacy. Whatever the source and accuracy of Graves's political history here, it seems clear that it was *The Golden Bough* which suggested the basic social realignment. Frazer summarizes a detailed argument by remarking that "the custom of brother and sister marriage in royal houses marks a transition from female to male descent of the crown." [27] Even Graves's choice of Hera seems partly conditioned by Frazer's having mentioned her in illustration of this practice.

In any event, this provides an additional complication in the

26. *The Greek Myths*, 1:50.
27. *Golden Bough*, 4:194.

thematic development of the last stanza. Hitherto, the poem was apparently following a ritual in the cyclic year of the White Goddess. But with this, clearly it is also rendering a crucial instant in human history by means of mythic fission. The night without the moon is no longer the monthly or octennial inter-lunar period which quickly yields to the return of the goddess and her consort. Now it is also the moment when the goddess suffers an historical eclipse from whose dreadful night Graves would say we are still struggling to free ourselves. Because the poem is set in history, it inevitably involves persons, real human beings. It is they and the poignancy of their disappearing love which invests the situation with more than narrative felicity. The plea "Dying sun, shine warm a little longer!" reverberates with the pitiful recognition that personal happiness as well as social and religious truths are subject to a dark, cold death that embraces the world as it is currently known and from which there may well be no release.

The same note of immediacy and personal sorrow for another human being's fate appears in "Intercession in Late October." It, too, is a poem functioning as a prayer, though in it the goddess is in the ascendance and the one to whom the request is made:

How hard the year dies: no frost yet.
On drifts of yellow sand Midas reclines,
Fearless of moaning reed or sullen wave.
Firm and fragrant still the brambleberries.
On ivy-bloom butterflies wag.

Spare him a little longer, crone,
For his clean hands and love-submissive heart.

The most striking thing about this poem, of course, is the use of Midas as a devoted hero and worshipper of the White Goddess. To contemporary minds at any rate, he has tradition-ally been taken as the awful lesson learned from a morality play disguised as myth and centering on vanity and greed. Graves, however, with some modest assistance from *The Golden Bough,*

sees in Midas not an avaricious fool but a king who heroically
faces his ritual death while continuing to enjoy life. Presumably
using facts such as that the name Midas was one of two born
by Phrygian kings in alternate generations and that he opposed
Apollo in choosing Marsyas as the winner of a musical contest
with the god, Graves extends or develops Frazer's points so that
Midas becomes a loyal follower of the goddess as vegetative
deity. He does so, Graves suggests, because she is his mother.[28]
Thus, although the image of "clean hands and love-submissive
heart" is clearly and primarily one of religious veneration, it is
perhaps striking that it should also match on a homely domestic
level the manner most pleasing in a child to its mother.

A significant difference between the two poems appears in
the techniques used to achieve the almost identical tone of
poignant entreaty mingled with stoical acceptance of the
inevitable. Unlike "Lament for Pasiphaë," this poem does not
comment on the protagonist's character or personality. Instead
it makes him a still, silent, reclining figure whose position is
defined and commented on by images from nature possessing
precise symbolic meanings. The first line of the poem establishes
the mythic station of the year while in Frazerian fashion stressing
its living quality that makes it an apt and touching analogy of
the human condition. The next line further narrows the focus
of the poem to one portion of the myth, that period in which
Midas is ridding or has just ridden himself of his golden curse
by ritually bathing in a river in accordance with the god's
instructions. The point would seem to be that since he has been
obedient to the divine instructions and been rewarded with
purification, he need not fear the imminent future and the end
of the year or any other disaster in the course of his life. Hence
he is, as befits the genuine pleasure-lover, unmoved by the
threats of death and gossip or scandal that are implicit in the
moaning reed and the sullen wave. They do, it is true, symbolize
both the reed that divulged Midas's secret of the ass's ears and

---

28. *The White Goddess*, p. 302. He also claims Midas worships Dionysus and so follows
his sources as well, providing an explanation of the ass's ears Midas acquires.

the last two months of the ancient year when everything is turning deathward. Yet such future disasters are offset by the flourishing of the brambleberries and the flowering of the ivy, both of which Graves asserts in *The White Goddess* are sacred to Dionysus and Osiris, the signs of the tenth and eleventh months when revelry and joy honor the god, and the symbols of resurrection and poetic inspiration.[29] Thus, in elaborate natural symbolism these lines combine to say that the time is not yet, though it is fast approaching.

Like Frazer, Graves here shows the emblematic quality of nature by means of which man understands and acquiesces in his lot through seeing it as a reflection and ritual miming of divine existence. For both, there is an unmistakable sense in which nature is not only the ultimate ground of life but also the archetypal form it possesses. To see the natural world as alive and fecund is to see it either as a garden or a woman, and it is in these guises that nature appears to Frazer and Graves respectively. If Graves's goddess frequently seems to resemble a Blakean Rahab, then just as much does Frazer's golden bough or sacred grove appear a Spenserian Garden of Adonis.

When Graves sees nature as a garden, it is more apt to be the treacherous Bower of Bliss. This is clearly borne out by "The Sirens' Welcome to Cronos," which views the Odyssean temptation as a version of the ritual course of the sacred king. Though death is the aim of the Sirens in Graves's poem as much as it is in Homer, the form the temptation takes has a different emphasis. While Homer does allude to the flowery meadow in which they sing, it is the power of sound that holds the real threat. Graves, on the other hand, makes the sensory appeal primarily visual and tactual, both of which are made to emphasize the natural setting in such a way that nature appears as a soft, enveloping, protective body warding off all physical and emotional pain and distress. In short, it offers to function as a second womb. Their Silver Island is covered with alder-wood that makes the Sirens invisible, "hid in a golden haze." And

29. Ibid., pp. 189-91, 221-22.

blossoming wild apples merge with the alders and silver firs to provide a backdrop for the wrens playing in their branches. Even the Sirens themselves, who naturally look like the White Goddess since they are versions of her and serve as her priestesses, are presented in similes grounded in natural symbolism:

> Our hair the hue of barley sheaf,
> Our eyes the hue of blackbird's egg
> Our cheeks like asphodel.

But that this scene is one of death for the god and his representative is clear even apart from the Homeric parallel. The fact that the "Wrens in the silver branches play / And prophesy you well" tells us the protagonist is doomed even though the Sirens protest that "No grief nor gloom, sickness nor death, / Disturbs our long tranquility; / No treachery, no greed." For as Graves learned from *The Golden Bough*, the wren who is hunted at Christmas time symbolizes the spirit of the old year and the one who kills him is his successor and called the king.[30] In the light of this, the stanza containing a frank offer of sexual pleasure with the Sirens takes on the character of ritual entertainment provided the sacrificial victim. An equally subtle fusion of allurement and warning, of offer and threat, occurs in the final stanza which shifts the attention from the pleasures of nature to the satisfaction of ambition and aspiration:

> A starry crown awaits your head,
> A hero feast is spread for you:
> Swineflesh, milk and mead.

As the ancient myths make clear, man must first be dead to escape the common human fate of being forgotten by being visibly enshrined in the heavens. Hence the starry crown holds out the promise of renown beyond the ordinary measure but

30. Ibid., pp. 192-93; cf. *Golden Bough*, 8:317-21.

at the cost of death. The same point is made with the allusion
to the hero feast, for as Graves knows from his reading of
Jane Harrison, such feasts commemorate the man who is dead.[31]

While there is a certain amount of duplicity in the Sirens'
offers, it is no more than is appropriate to the blandishments of
the temptress. A more sustained and shocking kind of female
deception, which nevertheless Graves extenuates, is presented
in "The Jackals' Address to Isis." This poem directs both
commiseration to and accusation at Isis over the death and
dismemberment of her husband Osiris. The gist of the argument
is that Isis herself tempted Set, Osiris's antagonist, to murder her
husband. Therefore her mourning is not an expression of grief
so much as an effort "to pacify the unquiet ghost." What is
significant here is less Graves's use of specific points found in
Frazer, like the five intercalary days alluded to in the final lines
of the poem, than the revolutionary reinterpretation he gives the
myth of Osiris and Isis. From a model of fidelity and marital
devotion he transforms it into a variant of the archetypal story
of the White Goddess who both loves and sacrifices her consort.
Like Frazer, though in more extreme form, he claims to be
arriving at a truth that has been both buried and willfully
distorted. At the same time, the purpose of his exposure is not
to heap moral obliquity on the head of Isis and, by extension,
womankind but rather to exalt her through a feeling of
compassionate awe in the face of the truth:

> "What harder fate than to be woman?
> She makes and she unmakes her man."

The Frazerian cycle of birth and death, fertility and sterility in
nature, is here augmented by an emphasis on creation and
destruction. What redeems both Frazer's nature and Graves's
woman from any Tennysonian charges of wanton cruelty is the
clear sense of their operating inevitably and in accord with laws

---

31. Harrison, *Prolegomena*, pp. 349-62; Harrison, *Themis*, pp. 307-16.

which man personalizes and in some measure humanizes through embodying them in ritual.

In the final two poems of the section Graves presents a segment of archetypal history which explains and justifies the goddess's ostensible savagery. The first of these, "The Destroyer," is a satire aimed at Perseus, "the man," Graves claims, "who first tilted European civilization off balance, by enthroning the restless and arbitrary male will under the name of Zeus and dethroning the female sense of orderliness, Themis." [32] This mythical figure has an historical form too, for Perseus is said to figure "the breaking of the Argive Triple Goddess's power by the first wave of Achaeans." [33] What the poem does, in effect, is to personify history as a hero thereby achieving greater compression and immediacy. The features of Perseus's nature that are singled out for attack, then, are an adroit combination of the personal and the cultural: narrowness that makes for invincibility; presumptuousness that uses sexuality as a weapon rather than an offering; folly that is indifferent to the core of human life—family and food; and ignorant acquisitiveness that has no sense of its own danger.

Though the goddess has been displaced and despoiled of her worship and fertility, she nevertheless can take an icy amusement from her knowledge of the debasement of her rites and of her ultimate restoration:

> Gusts of laughter the Moon stir
> That her Bassarids now bed
> With the ignoble usurer
> While an ignorant pale priest
> Rides the beast with a man's head
> To her long-omitted feast.

Like Frazer, Graves concentrates a certain amount of his fire

32. The White Goddess, p. 540.
33. Ibid., 245.

on Christianity and its deliberate ignorance of its origins. And like Eliot, he excoriates the transformation of sex from a religious ritual into a commercial enterprise.

The amusement inspired in the moon-goddess is due not only to the contrast between the matriarchal past and the patriarchal present but also to her knowledge that ultimately she will come again. The form that her resurrection and reassertion of power takes is symbolized through a multileveled natural world in the "Return of the Goddess." The dramatic tension throughout is achieved by setting the frogs, who know her return is fore-ordained, over against the rest of nature, which serves to presage that return. This is seen most sharply in the first stanza:

> Under your Milky Way
> And slow-revolving Bear
> Frogs from the alder thicket pray
> In terror of your judgement day,
> Loud with repentance there.

The astronomical references, as *The White Goddess* confirms, both identify the goddess as Rhea and locate her at the still point in the turning world. Though distant, the mother goddess inexorably approaches to reassert her authority over the universe that is hers. The prospect of her return is an awesome one for those who have denied her godhead and submitted to her male rival. In symbolizing such persons as frogs, Graves would seem to be drawing on their roles in *The Golden Bough* as well as the natural repugnance their image engenders. Their small size, loathsome appearance, and lack of power merge with Frazer's point about their being transmigrated sinners and the cause of death to provide that interpenetration of natural and mythic Graves desires.[34] And that their terror and belated repentance is not unwarranted we shall recognize when the third stanza is seen in the light of *The Golden Bough*.

First, however, we must note the way in which the second

---

34. *Golden Bough*, 8:299; Frazer, *The Belief in Immortality*, 1:61-62.

stanza advances the return of the goddess and underscores its imminence:

> The log they crowned as king
> Grew sodden, lurched and sank;
> An owl floats by on silent wing
> Dark water bubbles from the spring;
> They invoke you from each bank.

Each of the images—the sunken log, the silent owl, and the dark water—symbolize not so much the goddess as the fate of her antagonist and the conditions which make her return imminent. The log crowned as king is clearly derived from the yule log so thoroughly described by Frazer. It was the prime object in the midwinter fire festivals of ancient times, and, as Frazer's accounts show, was the vegetative form in which the god appeared whose birthday was the winter solstice. Its function was purificatory in that its fire was capable of destroying all evil things, particularly witches, but at the same time, it possessed protective and fructifying powers.[35] *The Golden Bough* does not really discuss the immersion and sinking of the log as part of the ritual, though there are hints that truncated and symbolic versions of this were observed. Nor does the poem follow Frazer's stress on the beneficent properties of the log. Graves, however, is not contradicting Frazer so much as he is augmenting him. Thus, the sinking of the crowned log clearly represents catastrophe for its worshippers. Since it is a substitute for the sacred king and god, the catastrophe in question is just as clearly the death of the male figure whose rites bulk so large in *The Golden Bough* and behind which stand the ritual patterns of the female deity Graves calls the White Goddess.

The submersion of her upstart antagonist is followed by the owl's flight. Graves invests this creature with its traditional attribute of wisdom, but he also follows *The Golden Bough* in making it emblematic of women and the guardian spirit or soul

---

35. *Golden Bough*, 10:246-69.

of a tree.[36] The upshot of this welter of anthropological lore is that the owl's appearance marks the death of the god, which in turn confers on the archetypal woman the wise realization of the fruitful nature of death and destruction. That the goddess is inevitably linked with these last is borne out by the dark water from the spring. It reminds us of the Orphic black spring of forgetfulness even as its color bespeaks the goddess under her death aspect. And back of this may stand Frazer's points about water being the destructive repository of objects symbolizing tree spirits and about a figure named Death which stands for the old year and winter.[37]

From this it is clear that Graves sees in the goddess's return not the simple restoration of fertility and a golden age at which all can rejoice but a time of waste, terror, and destruction that must inevitably accompany the change of any order. That the goddess's cruelty aims to bring her world back once again into the proper alignment with her own person is tersely but touchingly evident from the final stanza:

> At dawn you shall appear,
> A gaunt red-legged crane,
> You whom they know too well for fear,
> Lunging your beak down like a spear
> To fetch them home again.

The crane, according to *The White Goddess*, is associated with the poet and literary secrets so that here Graves seems to be suggesting that the goddess is not merely the symbol of an ancient religion and of nature itself but also of the source of poetic inspiration. *The White Goddess* also reveals Graves's familiarity with Frazer's comments about the crane serving as a signal for the commencement of the autumnal sowing of grain. Therefore, we may surmise that he was aware too of Frazer's identification of the crane as an emblem of longevity.[38] Such a

---

36. Ibid., 2:142 n. 2; 6:111 n. 1; 9:202, 217-18.
37. Ibid., 2:75, 76; 4:234, 246.
38. Ibid., 7:45, and n. 1; 1:169 n. 1.

collocation of significance can mean only one thing. The goddess returns as the Muse, poetic power, who is so long-lived as to be immortal because she recognizes that fertility and fructification are contingent on violation and penetration. The fertility goddess whom the ploughman invokes demands that the earth be entered by the plow and the seed before she will confer her blessings. In the same fashion the crane plunges her beak into the frogs and other creatures to bring them through death once more into contact with the fructifying reality of her godhead.

The reality dealt with here, however, is more than that of the natural world; it is also that of the imaginative world. The crane as Muse symbolizes in her dramatic ritual of fishing that poetry is not simply celebratory but is also critical. It is satiric as well as lyric and as such is a power of awesome proportions in the ordinary world of human affairs. As poems like "Traveller's Curse after Misdirection" and comments in *The White Goddess* and elsewhere make clear, Graves is avowedly following a Celtic tradition according to which satires by a true poet were capable of working actual physical harm on the person attacked. But in view of the range of his anthropological knowledge, the linking of satire and cursing may be traced to *The Golden Bough* and the works of Jane Harrison. Both point out that curses are frequently part of public rituals aimed at achieving beneficent results.[39] Harrison, in particular, provides a paradigm of the relation between Graves's ambivalent goddess and literary modes when she remarks that "the ritual of expulsion, riddance, cursing and finally purification issues in the literature of blame, the ritual of induction, of blessing, of magical fertilization in the literature of praise."[40] Both together constitute a unity, she suggests, for though they are valid distinctions, "at bottom is the one double-edged impulse, the impulse towards life."[41] In the light of this, the goddess as crane and the muse of satire impales her victims less from a sense of personal revenge than as a means of reestablishing her authority and of bringing

39. Ibid., 1:45, 279 ff; Harrison, *Prolegomena*, pp. 138-45.
40. Harrison, *Epilegomena to the Study of Greek Religion* (New York: University Books, 1962), p. xix.
41. Ibid., p. xix.

home to the world the fact that she is its ruler. Death, then, becomes a force and a means through which the inviolable order of life is asserted and recognized.

## IV

So far, attention has been focused primarily on the White Goddess, her development as a distinct figure and her ritual patterns. As Graves suggests, she appears as both a triad and a pentad as do her rituals and her male associates. Thus, at the risk of some simplification, we can see that in the nature-human-divine complex she appears variously as mother, beloved, muse, slayer, and burier while her male complement plays the roles of son, lover, poet, victim, and hero. And in playing these various roles, they both dramatically participate in the rituals which are essentially those of birth, sex, trancelike inspiration or vision, death, and resurrection seen as an act of memory. But not all of Graves's attention is explicitly and exclusively focused on her nature and accomplishments. Thus, when he looks at the male, he is most likely to see him as a human victim whose contact with divinity comes through his role as Frazer's tempo-rary king, reigning briefly and then being killed when the real ruler is ready to assume the throne once again. Such, of course, is the image that dominates, as we have seen, "Intercession in Late October." There Midas the victim was simply an object, a creature silently engrossed in his own existence. Consequently, the emotional response was engendered by the choruslike narrator who intercedes with the goddess on his behalf. In poems like "The Young Cordwainer," "Darien," and "Dethrone-ment" the victim plays a larger, more dramatic, and more lifelike part, and at the same time illuminates the significance of the total role.

The logically prior of these three poems is "Darien," for it deals both with the victim and with the conception of the goddess's child. The poem takes the form of a father's retro-spective account of his son and of how he came to marry the youth's mother. Investing this with archetypal significance is the

fact that the woman is both "the one Muse" and the moon-
goddess prepared to give birth to the new sacred king at the
winter solstice. Similarly the ritual's being one of passion,
conception, birth, death, and resurrection is clear from the
collocation of symbolic images like the heather-tree, the king-
fisher, the double axe, and the cockle-shell.[42]

More important, however, is the manner in which the courtship proceeds. Though the danger inherent in the goddess is not
ignored—"a cold shudder shook me / To see the curved blaze
of her Cretan axe"—her meeting with Darien's father suddenly
reveals her as a shy, unhappy creature caught in the meshes of
her role and so pitifully defenseless as to move her newfound
lover to a like sadness:

> No awe possessed me, only a great grief;
> Wanly she smiled, but would not lift her eyes
> (As a young girl will greet the stranger).

Ruling her mind is the great female impulse for offspring. This
result of their marriage is her sole concern and a necessary
condition for its occurrence:

> . . . If I lift my eyes to yours
> And our eyes marry, man, what then?
> Will they engender my son Darien?

And though the child is as yet neither conceived nor born, she
nevertheless describes him and his role of "Guardian of the hid
treasures of your world." At this point, her lover recognizes and
in so doing accepts the ultimate fate to which his love will
bring him. The symbol of this is his self-identification with
Orpheus as the oracular victim of devotion. To be a victim of
the goddess is no mere personal indulgence in the possible
disasters of romantic love. It is a solemn duty arising out of a
grave cultural crisis:

42. *The White Goddess*, pp. 193-94, 200; *Golden Bough*, 5:134, 163, 182-83; 9:269.

> . . . the times are evil
> And you have charged me with their remedy.

As the poet sees it, the remedy is clearly to mate with the goddess so that Darien his successor may be born and resurrect the age. As the child of the goddess, he assumes all the attributes connected with her domain and in so doing becomes the consummate epitome of Frazer's reviving god and his human counterpart, the sacred king:

> He is the northern star, the spell of knowledge,
> Pride of all hunters and all fishermen,
> Your deathless fawn, an eaglet of your eyrie,
> The topmost branch of your unfellable tree,
> A tear streaking the summer night,
> The new green of my hope.

In this complex, knowledge, action, and existence are interrelated so as to reveal them as all aspects of the goddess's one great love, her offspring.

But to see the poem as simply a dramatic dialogue from a mythical past or even as a symbolic declaration of the proper relation of man to woman is to ignore both the Orphic identification of the poet and the goddess's role as Muse. Ultimately, Graves is concerned here with defining the true poet and the relation he must have to inspiration or the craft of poetry. The true poet knows the hardships and eventual annihilation stemming from the struggle with poetic language and yet eagerly accepts the destruction of his own self in order that a new and better creature, an eternal being, a poem, may be born. Seen in this light, "Darien" is neither so remote from the present nor so quixotically literal in its elevation of woman to a position of absolute authority. Instead it is an extended and multileveled metaphor for the making of a poem, a metaphor whose terms are drawn from the elemental world of *The Golden Bough* and whose inception is the result of the interaction of the minds of Graves and Frazer.

"The Young Cordwainer" also deals with lovers and the intermingling of fear and desire that makes up the sealing of their love, but here the emphasis is quite different. For one thing, the poetic form is roughly that of a ballad with the lovers speaking antiphonally as they move through a dark mansion, up a large stairway whose foot is adorned with carved mastiffs, and into a locked bedroom containing "the state bed." For another, the characters are fully human rather than supernatural and the setting is loosely historical instead of mythical. In short, what Graves concentrates on here is the ritual of the goddess as it is enacted unwittingly by persons who may never have heard of her but who nevertheless testify by their actions to her power.

As if to point up their artlessness, he reverses their initial relationship from that of the goddess and her lover. Now it is the woman who is timorous and critical in a way that underscores her femininity and helplessness, while the man is consoling and purposeful. The core of the drama is the loss of desire or passion on the part of the woman and the man's endeavor to cope with this situation. He does so, however, in a manner diametrically opposed to what the bulk of the poem would lead us to expect. For in leading her "To this lampless hall, / A place of despair and fear / Where blind things crawl" and declaring that "Primrose has periwinkle / As her mortal fellow," he would seem to be preparing to kill her. In fact, as the final stanza and a half show us, it is he who is going to die at the hands of his beloved, thereby completing the ritual of the goddess correctly.

For our purposes this poem has two important qualities. The first is that it shows the goddess and her pattern being divested of its ancient setting and supernatural characters. It is stripped of all that sets it off from the immediacy of contemporary life. While the ballad is obviously not modern in form, it does have the same skill in using symbols of such simplicity and diction of such dreamlike clarity as its Tudor and Renaissance predecessors and models. Such an achievement invests even the ostensibly most artless surface with a haunting resonance. Graves fastens on the ballad as the medium best fitted to convey the archetypal or perennial nature of the theme. At the same time, the ballad form tells a modern audience that the narrative may or perhaps must have metaphoric irradiations from its own concentric statements. Thus, the wine-drugged lover slain amid the torpor of gratified sensuality is more than a story of what may have happened in the legendary past. It is also a metaphor of the ending of love in any time.

Such a metaphor is more than merely descriptive, it is educative in that it embodies a living ritual for terminating a dying love affair. What makes it living is that it is a matter of personal discipline and psychological maturity. The lover does not attempt to revive the passion of an earlier day, neither does he cajole, accuse, or plead. He is content merely to present the mythic image for the beloved to interpret and so to transform her own initial arch temptation, to prolong the relationship into the determination to end it with equal dignity:

> SHE: Love, have you the pass-word,
> Or have you the key,
> With a sharp naked sword
> And wine to revive me?
>
> HE: Enter: here is starlight,
> Here the state bed
> Where your man lies all night
> With blue flowers garlanded.
>
> SHE: Ah, the cool open window
> Of this confessional!
> With wine at my elbow,
> And sword beneath the pillow,
> I shall perfect all.

The ending of a love is, Graves suggests, a kind of death, one that decimates he who is still enraptured. For all that it need not and should not be other than a ceremonial testimony to the power of love to realize its own complete nature: "I shall perfect all." In the mouth of the woman, this statement is an ominous threat against her lover's life. On the lips of the goddess, it is an assertion of her own cycle of existence in which all things, even love, are born, flower, and perish. Hence to seek to avoid it is as churlish as it is foolish.

On turning to "Dethronement" one's first feeling is that Graves is rather sharply contradicting the views developed in "Darien" and "The Young Cordwainer." The former presents the victim as a kind of Keatsian voluptuary half in love with his own destruction. The latter shows a restrained, dignified accepter of his fate. In both cases the emphasis is on reaching out to embrace the encounter with death. "Dethronement," however, appears to reverse this perspective even as its setting returns to the mythic. The victim is enjoined to observe the goddess:

> . . . how she enacts her transformations—
> Bitch, vixen, sow—the laughing, naked queen
> Who has now dethroned you.

Then he is to flee wildly when her performance ends so that her Hounds of Hell and she may have the sport of pursuing and slaying him:

> Run, though you hope for nothing: to stay your foot
> Would be ingratitude, a sour denial
> That the life she bestowed was sweet.
> Therefore be fleet, run gasping, draw the chase
> Up the grand defile.

> They will rend you to rags assuredly
> With half a hundred love-bites—
> Your hot blood an acceptable libation
> Poured to Persephone, in whose domain
> You shall again find peace.

Here the victim will be indistinguishable from the terror-stricken beast of prey save for the spirit in which he enacts his hopeless part in this Darwinian ritual of the struggle for survival. And yet even in this Graves finds a mode for unservilely worshipping the goddess who brings birth, love, and death:

> Hymns to her beauty or to her mercy
> Would be ill-conceived. Your true anguish
> Is all that she requires. . . .

To treasure life passionately and to struggle, however vainly, against its termination shows the goddess the exalted value one places on her gift better than the litanies of praise and prayer found in "The White Goddess" and "Intercession in Late October."

Yet as the last stanza ("They will rend you to rags assuredly") indicates, the contorted agonies of flight from death are not the final image in which the human struggle culminates. The terror, pain, and anguish endured in the throes of death do not last. They are but a sacrificial rite of transition and of what Jane Harrison calls tendance or service to the deity. When one is dead, they are past; finally the goddess provides man with peace. It is significant that here her final form should be that of Persephone. As we have seen, Graves, with the aid of *The Golden Bough*, equates her with vegetative fertility as well as with the maiden consigned by love to live with death. This identification of the goddess together with the description of death by dismemberment as "love-bites" clearly indicates that the victim is the prey of love as well as death. In short, the peace before him is less that of personal serenity than the tranquillity found in the transformation of consciousness into a mute fertilizing agent. Thus, as in "Instructions to an Orphic Adept," Graves turns the ostensible profferment of personal immortality into an ironic disclaimer of it. At the same time this becomes a defense of the limited but more authentic virtues of eternal mortality. In this regard the metaphors of flight, pursuit, love-bites, and libations are not palliatives disguising unpleasant reality but explorations of the interrelation of death with life so that the discomforts of the one are assuaged by the truth of the other.

# CHAPTER IV

# The Rituals of Nature

As we have seen, the victim's role is neither simple nor confining, at any rate, no more than life itself. Sacred king, poet, lover, the hunted, all are defined through their actions and transcended through their capacity for wisdom. Substantially the same complex freedom and achieved insight characterizes those poems which focus on what might be broadly called phallic or fertility rituals rather than on the nature of the goddess and her consort. In all of these, love as expressed in sexuality is the point of attraction or repulsion that shapes the thematic development.

One of the earliest of these, written when Graves avowedly was influenced by Freudian views, is "The Bedpost." This is a kind of nursery rhyme about a little girl's being entertained with "stories of old battle / As she lies in bed," stories told her by "the post and ball / Of her sister's wooden bedstead / Shadowed on the wall." The interesting thing about this poem is not really its obvious Freudian allegory but rather its displacement of sexual fantasies into a world of legend. The existence of sexuality prior to one's consciousness of it is, of course, an important psychological and sociological phenomenon. Of more importance for our purposes is the fact, dramatically developed here, that the child's oblique approach to sexuality is so often via legend, myth, and literature. And while Frazer refused to read Freud, nevertheless *The Golden Bough* exhibits in prolific detail the impingement of sex upon myths and legends of all races and times. Indeed, perhaps its most central thesis is quite simply that all of man's activities—religious, economic, social—are dedicated to the ensuring of fertility both human and vegetative.

This theme becomes increasingly explicit in the course of the poem. Beginning with godlike warrior parents, a treacherous sea king, and heroic children, the poem in fairy tale fashion moves on to an amorous princess and a vengeful witch who transforms a hero into the bedpost until released by the pity of a maiden. Vigorous action, ego-gratifying fantasies, romantic projections of love and marriage, all culminate in the covert recognition of love as necessarily sexual if it is to be truly emancipatory. But from the acceptance of this the child shies away in favor of the military violence which symbolically rejects and represses the phallic world:

> But Betsy likes the bloodier stories,
> Clang and clash of fight,
> And Abel wanes with the spent candle—
> "Sweetheart, good night!"

The phallic ritual is avoided out of preference and a dim sense of fear in "The Bedpost." In "The Bards" and "A Jealous Man" it is touched upon as a way of defining emotions and revealing the nuances of passion. The first of these poems describes medieval bards fumbling their performance because "a something fearful in the song / Plagues them." The cause of their troubles is "an unknown grief" resident in their art form. In its raw power and crude insistence this grief is likened to a savage giant ravaging a genteel court:

> . . . a churl
> Goes commonplace in cowskin
> And bursts unheralded, crowing and coughing,
> An unpilled holly-club twirled in his hand,
> Into their many-shielded, samite-curtained,
> Jewel-bright hall where twelve kings sit at chess
> Over the white-bronze pieces and the gold;

And by a gross enchantment
Flails down the rafters and leads off the queens—
The wild-swan-breasted, the rose-ruddy-cheeked
Raven-haired daughters of their admiration—
To stir his black pots and to bed on straw.

The point here is just the reverse of that in "The Bedpost,"
where the phallic pattern was concealed and presented in terms
of other stories. Here the motif of sexual capture and enslavement is explicit and used to define in dramatic terms an emotion
that is common but without cause. At the same time, the extension of the simile allows us to read it not only as a kind of
psychological allegory but also as a revelation of the roots sex
has in physical violence and imaginative power. And out of
these two aspects of the simile we grasp the similarity of outer
and inner worlds, of their subjection to a logic which in both
cases admits only of its own need or desire.

A similar treatment of the battle of the sexes occurs in "A
Jealous Man," which presents the shaping impact of the emotion
on an individual's perceptions of the relations between the sexes.
To the jealous person with "a mind dream-enlarged" the sexuality
of others appears as

. . . warfare,
Man with woman, hugely
Raging from hedge to hedge:

The raw knotted oak-club
Clenched in the raw fist,
The ivy-noose well flung,

The thronged din of battle,
Gaspings of the throat-snared,
Snores of the battered dying.

To such an exaggerated vision sexuality, war, and death constitute both a series of images whose deepening significance

reflects the growing intensity of his passion and also a sequential definition of the existential meaning of "man with woman."

The paradigmatic image of that relationship is the one of oak-club and ivy-noose, suggesting the balanced nature of the contest, while the antiquity of these terms underscores the perennial character of the struggle. Significantly enough, Graves turns to vegetative symbolism with deep anthropological and mythological roots to convey his lively appreciation of the tension endemic to male-female relations. In *The White Goddess* he suggests that medieval carols traditionally juxtaposed the holly and ivy to represent the domestic war of the sexes and that holly and oak are both rivals and substitutes.[1] In effect, both in it and the poem, he regards these trees as symbolizing man and woman respectively but under their mythic forms of Dionysus and the Bacchanals. Consequently, the jealous man, writhing over the possibility that his beloved has or will enact the love battle to the death with someone other than him, ritualistically enacts the truth of the Dionysian myth with its consummation through destruction of the lover. At this point one recalls both Frazer's attention to the myth and the elaborate wealth of detail he provides concerning the ritual symbolism of the oak as well as his linking of the ivy with other dying gods besides Dionysus. In context, then, it seems more than likely that *The Golden Bough* materially shaped Graves's effort here to project the psyche of the individual living out its jealous passion into the archetypal world of dying gods and eternal goddesses.

In the preceding examples, the phallic ritual or myth has been the medium of illustrating or developing the theme, but in "Leda" theme and myth are coterminous. Like Yeats, Graves focuses exclusively on the mating aspect of the myth. His imagination is impelled by the beauty-and-the-beast motif, by the idea of and implications in sexual relations between a human being and an

---

1. *The White Goddess*, pp. 185-87, 190. Though the poem antedates *The White Goddess*, it is likely that this kind of information was known by Graves as early as 1927, when he published *The English Ballad, a Short Critical Survey* (London: Ernest Benn Ltd., 1927).

animal. Yet the poem is not contemplative in character; it is a dramatic lyric in which the poet speaks directly to the heart, which he accuses of "bawdry, murder and deceit" and relates to Leda. By focusing primarily on the heart rather than Leda, the author reveals the psychological character of his attitude toward the myth. He examines the emotions generated by a contemplation of Leda's mating and characterizes the nature of their source. Thus, the first two stanzas deal with the primary and secondary reactions of the heart or imagination to "That horror with which Leda quaked / Under the spread wings of the swan," whereas the final stanza diagnoses the cause of their appearance. This psychological exploration takes on a more analytic character when we notice that the poet addresses not *the* heart, not the organ common to all mankind, but rather simply "Heart," suggesting that it is his own he is concerned with. The more familiar, intimate form of address indicates that what follows is analogous to the psychoanalytic discovery of one's own most intimate secrets, secrets hitherto hidden even from oneself.

A brief lyric focusing on a single action in order to find parallels to other facets of human life must employ a language that is both highly figured and also condensed. Consequently, Graves's basic rhetorical devices are simile and metaphor, the former providing the parallels, the latter the condensation. They either create through symbolic appositeness a myth implicit in the texture of the poem or else, as here, play around one explicitly given so as to provide either a commentary on or a new use for it. Significantly enough, however, he begins the poem, in the first stanza, with statements of a reflective and contemplative character:

> Heart, with what lonely fears you ached,
> How lecherously mused upon
> That horror with which Leda quaked
> Under the spread wings of the swan.

From this scene, in which the heart is a spectator to Leda's fate, Graves then moves, by the use of metaphor, into a more immediate and dramatic image that identifies the heart or erotic imagination with Leda:

> Then soon your mad religious smile
> Made taut the belly, arched the breast,
> And there beneath your god awhile
> You strained and gulped your beastliest.

Thus the legend and Leda appear as psychological surrogates, as projections of private desires and impulses which are perpetuated because they have been objectified in the legend.

This is made explicit in the last stanza by the simile that identifies Leda and the heart through the qualities and behavior they have in common:

> Pregnant you are, as Leda was,
> Of bawdry, murder and deceit;
> Perpetuating night because
> The after-languors hang so sweet.

By these different rhetorical devices Graves gives us what are quite literally three different perspectives: first, the heart viewing Leda's experience from a distance; then, a close-up of the heart and Leda in which the one is superimposed on the other; and finally, the poet viewing both from the middle distance and pointing out their relationship. Through this technique Graves preserves the lyric's emphasis on both immediacy and insight.

Yet despite the poet's shrewd analysis and description, ambiguity is also central to the theme of the poem. It is, however, the ambivalence of the human heart, its ability both to lust for and to fear the same experience, rather than the erotic puzzle that dominates. At the outset the poet is struck by the heart's being beset by "lonely fears" at the same time as it "lecherously mused" upon Leda's fate. Its terrible secrets of "bawdry, murder and deceit" are kept because of the sensual pleasure provided by their recollection. Indeed, it is just this faculty of memory that dominates the entire poem and through the operation of its

various forms creates a present understanding of the heart's past
actions. In short, Graves here uses even more extensively than
before the ancient myth as mirror to the perennial ambivalences,
deceptions, and inconsistencies of human nature. The phallic
ritual repressed by Betsy and agonizingly endured by the jealous
man is with "Leda" an insanely depraved religious act, a descent
to literal bestiality in which pleasure outweighs fear and horror.

While "Leda" moves away from repression and violence as
responses to the phallic ritual, it still does not regard the rites of
love as ultimately desirable or inevitable. The full and frank
acceptance of sex as a ritual with supernatural dimensions occurs
only with two strikingly different poems, "Cry Faugh!" and
"To Juan at the Winter Solstice." The former is a witty
caricaturization of various historical and national attitudes
toward sexual love ranging from Platonic homosexuality to
modern scientific elimination of the issue. In the last two stanzas
the poet rejects all the solutions offered to "nymphological
disquiet" and proffers his own mythic answer:

> Cry faugh! on science, ethics, metaphysics,
> On antonyms of sacred and profane—
> Come walk with me, love, in a golden rain
>
> Past toppling colonnades of glory,
> The moon alive on each uplifted face:
> Proud remnants of a visionary race.

Philosophically, the argument is against any form of sexual
exclusion and for the celebration of a love invested with mythic
splendor. Mythically, it defines itself by an eclectic fusion of
Zeus's mating with Danae and Samson's destruction of the
temple. Significantly, the transition from clever irony to lyric
exaltation is effected through the allusive invitation "Come walk
with me, love" which draws both lover and beloved into the
world of myth.

What they confront there is not only their consummation
viewed as a natural event of great beauty but also the disastrous

consequences of a love that dares any and all risks. The soft delights and pleasures of love are balanced by the crashing destruction of a civilized splendor. This last both stands between man and the natural world and also interferes with his mythic communion with the white goddess. Thus the world of love, the phallic ritual, is as always for Graves a dual one of creation and destruction, of fulfillment and frustration. It is not, however, a world of escape, romantic or otherwise, for the time of myth as a paramount human mode is past. The lovers are simply "proud remnants of a visionary race" who share what remains with exaltation and face what is irretrievably lost, now or in the future, with stoic calm.

Such a view fully accepts the phallic ritual as humanly mean-ingful only in terms of a mythopoeic response and so accepts sex without either guilt or shame. Nevertheless, it is a kind of Arnoldian truncation both in its intimation that love is the only steadfast, trustworthy thing in life and in its hint that even so it is but a momentary stay against the confusion of the age. In "Cry Faugh!" the golden rain and living moon do not disguise the rejection implicit in the title and the destruction inherent in the toppling colonnades. Nor is any attempt made to hide the fact that sexual love unconfined by secular or religious prescriptions does not mesh with other forms of human order. This is the task, among many others, taken up by "To Juan at the Winter Solstice." What this poem, regarded by many as Graves's greatest, does is to integrate the phallic ritual into the total pattern of human existence which for the author is that provided by the White Goddess. It does so, however, not by providing it with a fixed place in the general scheme of things, for that would be but another type of exclusion limiting it in kind or scope.

Instead, the poet tells his young son:

> There is one story and one story only
> That will prove worth your telling,
> Whether as learned bard or gifted child;

To it all lines or lesser gauds belong
That startle with their shining
Such common stories as they stray into.

The logic of this, as the remainder of the poem demonstrates,
is that the phallic ritual is but a single form or version of the
one story and not a separate, self-contained incident in the
annals of humanity. Exactly the same impulses, actions, and
consequences occur in it as in the other forms. This is what
Graves bears in on his audience through the medium of poetic
structure. The five central stanzas substantially follow a single
principle of organization. The poet asks the child "Is it of this
you tell or this or this or this?" The specific topics mentioned
are substantially those dealt with in *The White Goddess*—tree
worship, the interpretation of strange azoological beasts, the
significance of the zodiac, the sacrificial victim, the ritual conflict,
and the service of the goddess. In each of the stanzas the final
emphasis falls on the ultimate fate of the protagonist, underscoring the fact that "there is one story and one story only,"
that of man's inevitable commitment to desire and endeavor and
its termination by his mortality.

This pattern of image and narrative illustrative of the same
point is also, strikingly enough, the same one as Frazer frequently
employs in *The Golden Bough*. For instance, his accounts of
dying gods deal not only with those of major cultures but also
include numerous instances of tribal chiefs and deities whose
rituals show substantial resemblances. The difference in scope
between *The Golden Bough* and the poem is, of course, that
between the epic and the lyric. Even so, in both the conclusion
is implied before it is ever stated by the succession of ostensibly
independent narratives and the selection of revelatory images.
This is not to say, of course, that Graves deliberately modeled
the poem on Frazer's method of organization. Yet Frazer has
had a powerful thematic and attitudinal influence on literary
artists, largely as a result of his having, apparently intuitively,
perceived the kind of organization post-nineteenth-century

studies must inevitably assume. Thus, at the very least Graves is clearly structuring his work in a fashion first exemplified by *The Golden Bough*.

It is in the fourth stanza, after the pattern of recurrence is well begun, that the phallic ritual is enunciated as an alternative for the putative taleteller:

> Or is it of the Virgin's silver beauty,
> All fish below the thighs?
> She in her left hand bears a leafy quince;
> When with her right she crooks a finger, smiling,
> How may the King hold back?
> Royally then he barters life for love.

The chief difference in this treatment of the theme from the previous poems is the illumination conferred through the context. Love had been seen before as beautiful, desirable, and inescapable, but only here does it appear as a complete human gesture or ritual. Here it is a participation not in a temporary scorning of the disability of one's mortal nature but in an eternal acceptance and fulfillment of human capacity. In sum, to participate in the phallic ritual is shown by this poem to be one form of matching desire and reality, of filling out totally what man can do with what he does do. The achievement lies in realizing the bounds of capacity, reaching them, and not futilely longing for impossible extensions.

At the same time, the poem makes clear that the alternatives cited are not really alternatives. The question of what story is told does not carry an "either/or" logic with it. The implicit answer, as we can infer from *The White Goddess*, to the whole series of questions throughout the poem is always affirmative:

> Is it of trees you tell, their months and virtues,
> Or strange beasts that beset you,
>    Of birds that croak at you the Triple will?

Or of the Zodiac and how slow it turns
Below the Boreal Crown,
Prison of all true kings that ever reigned?

The child, like the poet himself, will tell all of these tales,
including that of the phallic ritual, during the course of his life,
and in doing so he will be telling "one story and one story only."
The unity of experience and vision gained by this realization is
threatened, as the zodiac image suggests, by the boredom of the
limited and predictable nature of life as seen from this perspective.

To face this threat and its companion—despair at the
inevitability of mortality—the last stanza offers an injunctive
commentary on the ritual cycle of action and narration presented
in the poem:

Dwell on her graciousness, dwell on her smiling,
Do not forget what flowers
The great boar trampled down in ivy time.
Her brow was creamy as the crested wave,
Her sea-blue eyes were wild
But nothing promised that is not performed.

The faintly liturgical quality of the opening lines exercises a
hypnotic emphasis on meaningful contemplation. It also stresses
the benevolence of the goddess not only in her self but in her
response to the inevitable death of her consort at the hands of
his antagonist. The despair at mortality is swallowed up by the
sense of confraternity in death conveyed in the image of the
destruction of vegetative beauty. Similarly, the boredom of the
predictability of death is relieved by the fascinated recognition
that even beauty and deity are not exempt from extinction. The
dual emphasis on the number and kind of individuals destroyed
is economically conveyed by the phrase "what flowers," which
carries the sense of the particular sort as well as the number of
flowers. The anemones of Adonis succinctly testify to the

prevalence of death. At the same time, their association with the
god reminds the listener that revivification of life is as inexorable
as its destruction.

The sole means to the achievement of this end is spelled out
in the challenge of divine beauty with which the poem concludes.
The untamed beauty of the goddess is rich with reward yet her
eyes promised nothing "that is not performed." Here again the
truth expressed is double-edged. On the one hand, she has
prophesied nothing that has not come about; she is, as it were,
the reality principle which squares possibility with actuality. On
the other hand, her creamy brow and wild eyes are an opaque
enigma offering nothing unless the individual first actively
achieves it himself. These two meanings are the matching halves
of the one story. The world including the human body, external
to the human consciousness, operates in accord with natural
laws, but at the same time yields enormous treasures to him
who acts with an understanding of how to use and to circumvent
individual laws. Thus, the goddess is nature viewed as the
total context in which man exists, and the poet is employing
the pattern of fertility myths described in *The Golden Bough* and
elsewhere to instruct his son in the only way of living in the only
world he personally will have.

## II

Though "To Juan at the Winter Solstice" may be the
quintessence of this education in the nature of the world, it is
not the whole of the learning process. An added part of it is the
informed ability to live in the natural world as well as the
capacity to cope with the threats and terrors of the other world,
which is inhabited by spirits and demons who threaten man
with the dislocation of his harmonious relationship with nature
and the goddess. One of the first requirements of human education in the myth of nature is to apprehend its relationship to the
nature of myth. Or, to put it less epigrammatically, the individual
must grasp something of the connections between nature and
deity.

An introduction to this topic occurs in the early poem

"Outlaws," which adumbrates in remarkably full fashion many of the themes and attitudes of those later works consciously shaped by *The White Goddess*. Opening in a scene of natural mystery complete with owls, darkness, and bats, the poem quickly establishes the identity and role of the outlaws:

> Old gods, tamed to silence, there
> In the wet woods they lurk,
> Greedy of human stuff to snare
> In nets of murk.

Nature, thus, is populated with deities anxious to entrap man in the toils of darkness. More important, however, than the danger they afford is their reason for doing so. Like Lawrence, Graves here insists that despite the decline and disappearance of ancient orthodoxies "These aged gods of power and lust / Cling to life yet." And in the balance of the poem he is primarily concerned with developing the contrast between their past eminence and present peripheral function:

> Old gods almost dead, malign,
> Starving for unpaid dues:
> Incense and fire, salt, blood and wine
> And a drumming muse,
>
> Banished to woods and a sickly moon,
> Shrunk to mere bogey things,
> What spoke with thunder once at noon
> To prostrate kings:
>
> With thunder from an open sky
> To warrior, virgin, priest,
> Bowing in fear with a dazzled eye
> Toward the dread East—

The burden of these lines closely resembles that at the close of *The White Goddess*. Both stress that unworshipped gods invoke their great powers against the disrespectful, exercising them in

the fiery Old Testament fashion of instant retribution and in
more subtle manners by letting the consequences of disrespect for
the sources of life work themselves out to their culmination in
sterility, madness, and death.

The precise forms in which retribution is exacted are not,
however, touched on here. The focus is on the resentment of the
gods and on the pathetic diminishment in their stature. The
function of this theme is not so much to offer a primitivistic
lament for the corruption of the modern world, though Graves
is not averse to such strictures, as it is to define the present
nature of nature. The world of nature, for Graves, is irremediably
anthropomorphic; as an organic entity, its animating force or
principles are the gods. And when the gods are diminished to
"living with ghosts and ghouls, / And ghosts of ghosts and last
year's snow / And dead toadstools," man is then moving in a
nature that is hostile and barren. He is sustained only by the
memory of a time when the ancient gods truly ruled man, who
out of fear, desire, and hope did them reverence. In calling up
such a memory, Graves, even in 1920 when this poem appeared
in *Country Sentiment*, seems to use *The Golden Bough* and Jane
Harrison's *Prolegomena* as handbooks of image and attitude.
The references to the gods' malignity, their speaking through
thunder, their singling out of king, warrior, virgin, and priest, and
their worship being a product of fear all clearly suggest this
relationship.

From such a situation the natural world and its human
inhabitants can move in two basic directions, each of which
opposes the other. The drift of "Outlaws" leads to "An English
Wood," where the diminution of power and lust result inevitably
in a nature "pledged / To the set shape of things, / And reason-
ably hedged." In contrast to a nature full of ancient gods
malignantly eager for the ritual sacrifices once made them, this
one is settled, serene, and predictable:

> Here nothing is that harms—
> No bulls with lungs of brass,
> No toothed or spiny grass,

> No tree whose clutching arms
> Drink blood when travellers pass,
> No mount of glass;
> No bardic tongues unfold
> Satires or charms.

It is the cultivated, civilized, rational nature of the English mind
which denies or eschews the awesome, sinister, magical universe
of the primitive mind such as that revealed by *The Golden Bough*.

Diametrically opposed to such a bland evaporation of nature
as a force to be placated is the attitude revealed in "Angry
Samson." Here man both uses and embodies in himself the
destructive powers of nature. He does so in order to affirm its
freedom from the constraints of seductive treachery and magical
rites. Samson is the human embodiment of uncontainable natural
energy asserting its own devastating power not for moral or
political reasons but as a way of affirming the autonomy of its
own laws and principles:

> O stolid Philistines,
> Stare now in amaze
> At my foxes running in your cornfields
> With their tails ablaze,
>
> At swung jaw-bone, at bees swarming
> In the stark lion's hide,
> At these, the gates of well-walled Gaza
> A-clank to my stride.

This is the antithesis of the passive nature of "An English Wood"
and the alienation of nature and deity in "Outlaws." Samson and
the natural world are exactly matched as we see from the dual
exhibition of destructive might by the foxes and Samson's club.

In *The White Goddess* Samson is identified with that type of
Hercules who is a Frazerian pastoral sacred king.[2] Since Samson,

---

2. *The White Goddess*, pp. 123-26. Graves also identifies him as a sun-hero (p. 140), a
view Frazer vigorously rejects in *Folk-lore in the Old Testament*, 3 vols. (London: Macmillan, 1919), 2:481, 482 n. 1.

especially as a lion killer, has long been a favorite of Graves, it would be difficult to assert categorically that he is given the same divine role in the poem. Nevertheless, in view of Graves's early interest in Frazer, it is worth noting that *The Golden Bough* does touch on Samson's trick with the foxes in its section on the corn spirit as fox.[3] And perhaps closer in tone and attitude to the poem is Frazer's account of Samson in *Folk-lore in the Old Testament.* There the sacred king aspect is replaced by a stress on "a real man, a doughty highlander and borderer, a sort of Hebrew Rob Roy, whose choleric temper, dauntless courage, and prodigious bodily strength marked him out as the champion of Israel in many a wild foray across the border into the rich lowlands of Philistia."[4] The only things, says Frazer, that redeem the story of Samson from the crassness and vulgarity of simple robbery and bullying are "the elements of supernatural strength, headlong valour, and a certain grim humour which together elevate it into a sort of burlesque epic after the manner of Ariosto."[5] And it is these same elements that figure so prominently in Graves's poem.

"Angry Samson" suggests that nature and its deity exact a violent revenge of the unbeliever. In turn "Ogres and Pygmies" stresses that vigor and fertility need have nothing to do with attractiveness let alone beauty whereas "Grotesques v" whimsically shows that such a power may be a grimly ironic comedian in his own right. The ogres are seen as monsters out of the past who become less repellent only in comparison to the effete weaklings of the present. They survive only as great neolithic statues worshipped with a mixture of awe and fear by country people who retain a sense of the monumental power they represent even as images. Through this version of the Battle between the Ancients and the Moderns, Graves underscores the necessity of coming to grips honestly with the problem of the vitality of raw primitive life, demanding candid apprecia-

3. *Golden Bough*, 7:297 n. 5.
4. Frazer, *Folk-lore, in the Old Testament*, 2:481.
5. Ibid.

tion while at the same time not losing sight of its shortcomings. In essence, the aim is to achieve a tension between the rival claims. This tension is not so much realized as lived, not so much psychological as physiological, absorbed into the living center of one's own being.

Both "Ogres and Pygmies" and "Grotesques v" are written with a gusto and rude humor that match their themes exactly. The latter, however, is more emphatically Frazerian or anthropological in matter. It is also a more amused exposition of what happens to man when his knowledge exceeds his piety in regard to natural religion. The Snake-god, whom we have met earlier in Graves's poetry, is here encountered by Sir John who approaches the deity "not as a votary" but with "somewhat cynical courtesy" despite the fact that "He was well versed in primitive religion." The god's response is to treat the snobbish, cultured, English gentleman first as a child to be entertained and then as a sacrifice to be eaten:

> The God was immense, noisy and affable,
> Began to tickle him with a nervous chuckle,
> Unfobbed a great gold clock for him to listen,
> Hissed like a snake, and swallowed him at one mouthful.

In their conclusions these two poems enunciate complementary but opposing positions. "Grotesques v" takes the wholly satiric, Popeian view in which the dunce not only reveals his folly but is destroyed by it without ever knowing why he has died. "Ogres and Pygmies," on the other hand, takes a more Rabelaisian view of the antagonists and stresses both the difficulty of decision and the access of insight that it conveys:

> And who would judge between Ogres and Pygmies—
> The thundering text, the snivelling commentary—
> Reading between such covers he will marvel
> How his own members bloat and shrink again.

The ultimate focus is on the reader rather than on either artist or critic. The reader embraces empathically the nature of both and so senses the need of contraries in any existential definition. Thus, the poem matches a limited and perhaps helpless knowledge against the ignorance of Sir John. In so doing it suggests that knowledge of nature and its deities is futile unless it is personally experienced. Such a view clearly implies that familiarity with *The Golden Bough*, for instance, is pointless if not augmented by the incorporation of its knowledge into one's own perspective. Thus, in a sense we see why *The White Goddess* came to be written: to adapt Frazer's and others' insights to the specific imaginative needs of Graves as a poet.

### III

All of the poems discussed so far have concentrated more on the nature deity and less on nature itself. Graves does, however, have a number of poems, perhaps one of his largest groups, which render nature immediately. Their greatest stress falls on its rhythms of fertility and sterility, its cyclical pattern of time and experience, and its assumption of human and divine form. In the case of this first motif, fertility and sterility, Graves presents a rather paradoxical nature. He suggests that nature is somehow preferable when it does appear sterile or at least infertile and barren. Thus, in "Rocky Acres" he points to the country of his choice as a wild land of mountains and moors, cold water, rocks and heather, and rapacious buzzards. And yet it is not an Eliotic wasteland, largely because it has its own productive effect on the protagonist:

> Tenderness and pity the heart will deny,
> Where life is but nourished by water and rock—
> A hardy adventure, full of fear and shock.

But this kind of world not only encourages toughness and resiliency, it also preserves a timeless realm "that rose from Chaos and the Flood." In it one can both stay clear of the effete, civilized society and also maintain undiminished contact with the man-gods of "the first land."

This tempering of the human soul through confrontation with a hard, intractable nature runs throughout many of Graves's poems, but it receives perhaps its most clear-cut expression in "The Rock at the Corner." This poem describes a rock left by quarrymen over which move "The comforting fingers / Of ivy and briar." The poet muses that it is in no real ultimate need of "nature's compassion" since it will starkly assume its role of guard against the ease of death:

> . . . travellers in winter
> Will know it for a creature
> On guard at the corner
> Where deep snows ingratiate
> The comforts of death.

Death is seen as the temptation to ease, comfort, renunciation of discipline and unrelenting effort, in short, as the cultivated landscape of the civilized world in "An English Wood." Many factors obviously go into the formation of such a view. One especially powerful element is likely the reading of *The Golden Bough* in which the painful yet unceasing struggle of primitive tribes to cling to life is called up in vivid and numerous scenes. Seeing in this the root nature of life, Graves may very likely have also found, as Frazer kept stressing, that the ostensibly and apparently futile ceremonies of magic and religious ritual were disciplined efforts to maintain life. In addition, they also preserved a kind of psychic autonomy and taut harmony or balance or tension between primitive, that is, basic or fundamental man and his universe.

From such a perception adapted to his own contemporary world, Graves was able to fashion poems celebrating a tough-minded acceptance of the unpretty, stark, violent dimensions of nature. In some sense these qualities correspond to the individual's states of critical desolation that he must learn to live

with if he is ever to overcome them. If he does not, he finds
himself in the world of death which in "It Was All Very Tidy"
is pictured as the owner of a universe very like that of "An
English Wood":

> When I reached his place,
> The grass was smooth,
> The wind was delicate,
> The wit well timed,
> The limbs well formed,
> The pictures straight on the wall:
> It was all very tidy.

Though the traditional symbols of natural and human
fertility are inadequate, as "Apples and Water" demonstrates,
this does not mean that they are to be avoided. The acceptance
of the nature of things is perhaps most thoroughly exemplified in
Graves's poems through the theme of love and the likelihood of
suffering and desolation it entails. Hence, as in "Sick Love," the
experience is urged on the individual even though it is
impermanent:

> O Love, be fed with apples while you may,
> And feel the sun and go in royal array.

While the *carpe diem* theme is prominent, more important is the
way in which the human being is drawn into and becomes part
of nature:

> Be warm, enjoy the season, lift your head,
> Exquisite in the pulse of the tainted blood,
> That shivering glory not to be despised.

> Take your delight in momentariness,
> Walk between dark and dark—a shining space
> With the grave's narrowness, though not its peace.

By accepting the rhythm of nature and celebrating its fructification and flowering in the human expression of life, the individual learns not simply his or her subjection to mortality but more importantly the value, beauty, and pleasure of the human season of fertility.

These things are not learned by simple, quasi-scientific observation or by a vaguely romantic identification of oneself with the surrounding environment. They are acquired rather by reading accurately what Graves calls the "Language of the Seasons." Such a language is spoken essentially in that nonurban world of agriculture which Frazer found to illuminate clearly the threats to survival as well as the magical rites with which to avoid them:

> Living among orchards, we are ruled
> By the four seasons necessarily:

In such a context, one learns the basic primitive language of human growth, flourishing, and decline:

> Framed love in later terminologies
> Than here, where we report how weight of snow,
> Or weight of fruit, tears branches from the tree.

The human relation so dear to romantics is here significantly resolved into a naturalistic equivalent of divine love. Like Frazer, Graves here secularizes a spiritual relation in order to reveal the fundamental ground of human existence as he sees it. The vegetative terminology of love is not merely a metaphor for the human passions; it is an account of the intimate interrelation subsisting between man and his world. The twin weights, of snow and fruit, bespeak obviously the two extremes of human love. Yet they also accurately render the polar emotions experienced by the person sensitive to the organic, living character of the natural world and the continuity of pattern it exhibits with the human being. *The Golden Bough* explores tree worship, including the notion of their marrying each other, with something of amused scientific superiority. Graves's poem, on the other hand, treats it as an illuminating image of the vicissitudes organic to love through the simple but daring expedient of transmuting the object of devotion.

This same metamorphic principle applied to the same subject is carried even further in "Lovers in Winter." It finds consolation for disappointment in love through the Frazerian identification of human and vegetative forms:

> The posture of the tree
> Shows the prevailing wind;
> And ours, long misery
> When you are long unkind.
>
> But forward, look, we lean—
> Not backward as in doubt—
> And still with branches green
> Ride our ill weather out.

The emblem of the tree and the winter suggests the seasonal character of love and by implication the cyclical pattern of nature, which, according to Graves, man must recognize as equally applicable to himself in the course of his life.

The correlation of natural and human cycles is explicitly made in the poem describing "The Finding of Love." In its inception love is seen to be "Pale at first and cold, / Like wizard's lily-bloom / Conjured from the gloom." Then, as it blossoms, it explodes in a profusion of natural emblems:

> Love dries the cobweb maze
> Dew-sagged upon the corn,
> He brings the flowering thorn,
> Mayfly and butterfly,
> And pigeons in the sky,
> Robin and thrush,
> And the long bulrush,

Bird-cherry under the leaf,
Earth in a silken dress,
With end to grief,
With joy in steadfastness.

In previous poems we have seen what might be called the naturalizing of man; here we witness the humanizing of nature by the traditional device of making earth a woman—a device of mythic origins as *The Golden Bough* demonstrates. It occurs also by presenting the animate and vegetative signs of spring and growth as visible expressions of love. The images from nature are largely the conventional ones of traditional nature poetry, of Georgian pastoralism crossed with Tudor lyricism. It is unlikely, however, that the freshness and direction of the imagery would have been so clear had not Graves absorbed Frazer's lesson. Both underscore the intimate identity of human and natural cycles and the value of a scrupulous attentiveness to the language of the seasons.

The ways in which the lessons of poetry and anthropology can be merged is suggested by "The Country Dance." Love as an imaginative and sexual passion is seen as a seasonal mood but a potentially dangerous one which can be overcome only by ritual expulsion. Thus, in the final stanza Graves concretizes the setting into that of a Tudor or early Renaissance setting. There the image of the dance takes on the Frazerian inflection of expressing the ritual fertility drama of primitive times. At the same time it is given an ironic note by likening love to illness rather than to health:

Leap high, jealous Ralph; jet it neat,
Merry Jill, and remove
By employment of elbows and feet
The green sickness of love.

The equating of the dance with love or courtship is a commonplace of any age, but this should not obscure Graves's remarkable originality, inspired by *The Golden Bough* and its general anthropological milieu. For him the dance is a ritual purgative or purifying agent that channels sexual ardor into quasi-athletic contests which in origin were imitative fertility rituals. And yet even here Graves may be stressing less the need of expelling love before it does any damage than the need of removing its unripe, green form. So viewed, the dance may be fulfilling its ancient, and contemporary, function of miming and so inciting fertility and growth. It ripens the green love through the competitive tensions of courtship expressed in rhythmic movement.

In any event, the conclusion of the preceding poem suggests that there are some dangers attendant on regarding love as a natural cycle and treating nature as a beautiful, gratifying, comforting creature whom one can love. This hint is made explicit in "A Love Story," which is perhaps the fullest account of the course taken by the cycle of love and nature. The speaker encounters a winter scene with full moon, recalling to him a similar experience as a boy in which he fell in love. But what makes this an archetypal experience in the Gravesian canon is the fact that it was the moon rather than a woman with which he fell in love:

> In boyhood, having encountered the scene,
> I suffered horror: I fetched the moon home,
> With owls and snow, to nurse in my head
> Throughout the trial of a new Spring,
> Famine unassuaged.
>
> But fell in love, and made a lodgement
> Of love on those chill ramparts.
> Her image was my design: snows melted,
> Hedges sprouted, the moon tenderly shone,
> The owls trilled with tongue of nightingale.

Love found in the time of desolation and barrenness is capable, as "Mid-Winter Waking" and "She Tells Her Love While Half

Asleep" also show us, of transforming entirely the world one feels and sees. But what this poem goes on to dramatize is the same thing *The Golden Bough* documents, namely, that the natural cycle leads from fulfillment and harvest to disillusionment and barrenness.

The moon begins to show signs of her role as white goddess when "her image / Warped in the weather, turned beldamish." As a result "back came winter on me at a bound." The moon is then revealed as Queen Famine, the ravening aspect of the White Goddess. It is here in the image of the moon that the human dimensions of nature crystallize for Graves. The moon is woman in the natural world, and it is because of this that she becomes the astronomical version of the White Goddess. Both are capable of consolation, pity, and love as well as indifference, cruelty, and destructiveness, as poems like "The Land of Whipperginny," "Full Moon," "To Lucia at Birth," and "Like Snow" demonstrate. The mystery, attractiveness, remoteness, and icy splendor of the moon mirror precisely the female and also define the natural world as it is apprehended by man. So that while Graves is talking much of the time about the relations of man and woman, he is also more obliquely but nevertheless tellingly exploring the relations of mankind to nature.

Existentialists inveigh against the bad faith of those who regard persons as objects. Graves by implication celebrates the magical faith implicit in seeing objects as persons. In doing so, however, he is not, like so many artists of the nineteenth century, sentimentally projecting his own feelings on to nature in order to magnify them. Rather, he is endeavoring to adapt to a modern setting the continuity and coherence of the primitive world-view as expounded by Frazer and others. The aim is a poetic cosmology that allows him a single, metaphor-based standard for describing and evaluating physical and psychological actions, events, and behavior. In this use of the ancient world revealed by *The Golden Bough*, Graves is one with many of the major figures in modern literature. They find in the myths and rituals of primitive peoples both images for poems and modes of ordering those images which will faithfully reflect their own outer and inner worlds.

The individual's education in nature entails a lively sense both of its benefits and of its dangers. This is nowhere better exemplified than in "To Lucia at Birth." The former is represented by "the moon beaming matronly and bland" as she greets all the newborn who enter her domain. Her amiable greeting is more than balanced, warns Graves, by her retinue:

> . . . her pale, lascivious unicorn
> And bloody lion are loose on either hand:
> With din of bones and tantarara of horn
> Their fanciful cortege parades the land—
> Pest on the high road, wild-fire in the corn.

By making the animal emblems of nature partly fanciful and partly real, Graves is indicating that the dangers of nature can be both existent and imagined. In the same way, when they appear as pest and wildfire, they are shown to be both naturalistic and mythopoeic. Gods and their antagonists were often presented in such guises, as Frazer's accounts of the mouse, locust, and mildew forms of Apollo and of the destructive effects of Samson's foxes make clear.

These dualities of reference underline the flexibility of forms in which they make their appearance. To view them as simply naturalistic or mythopoeic is to ignore their metamorphic power —their real danger, that of being unexpected, unrecognized, or unanticipated. The tension between the two modes prevents hypostatization, which would resolve nature into discrete elements and myth into fanciful tales long-since discarded as relevant only to the past. This same tension maintained in the poet's or speaker's own person is what motivates his warning to the infant:

> Then reckon time by what you are or do,
> Not by the epochs of the war they spread.

Hark how they roar; but never turn your head.
Nothing will change them, let them not change you.

Though one must enter into nature and recognize one's continuity with it, one must not, Graves suggests, surrender one's
autonomy as a distinct form of nature. Thus, human time is
different from natural time; the former is a matter of essence and
function, the latter of event. What matters most for man living
in and with nature is a clear grasp of his function as a human
being and of its difference from the functions of all other things
in nature. This is the burden of the last line. Underlying the
shifting, changing forms of nature is a substratum of unvarying
function which provides the coherence that allows us to think
of nature as a single unified system. Ritual seen as a recurring
pattern of meaningful action is therefore the archetype that
connects man and nature and which myths, such as that of the
White Goddess, record.

# CHAPTER V

# The Rituals of
# Dream and Language

The prime antagonist of human comprehension of nature, for Graves, is the demonic world whose external form is magic and whose internal form is dreams and nightmares. Like Lawrence and Charles Williams, Graves sees a kind of reality in the idea of a spirit world capable of imposing its own spells on the human perception of the natural universe. That reality, however, is largely psychological. The spirits are employed as literary conventions, especially in the earlier poems, which dramatize either contemporary experiences for which there is no other descriptive terminology or past beliefs whose pastness gives them a kind of reflective status that lets the reader grasp them as symbolic. A very early instance of this last is "The Haunted House" in which a bard offers his audience "clouded tales of wrong / And terror" drawn from the history of the house, tales of spirits and demons, of fear and lust and grief. The reader accepts the ballad convention but does so because he sees in the poem a perspective on his own world. Thus the poem ends:

> . . . What laughter or what song
> Can this house remember?
> Do flowers and butterflies belong
> To a blind December?

In so doing, it bears in on the reader the awareness that the tales of demons and spirits are verbal or literary analogues of specific human and natural cycles.

The demonic as a recurrent threat to man is rendered even more explicitly in "The Devil at Berry Pomeroy." Despite the jocularity of irregular dimeter couplets, it conveys a sharp sense of the perversion of the narrator's world by the intrusion of the Devil who "snaps his chain / And renews his reign." Landscape, vegetation, animal life, and human relations, all testify to his presence and rule: unseasonable weather, sickly children, unripened fruit, prevalence of witches and ghosts, monstrous births, blighted fields, murder, incest, and rape. Many of these features of the demonic or diabolic universe also testify to the shaping force of *The Golden Bough.* Such phenomena are described in vivid terms by Frazer. Furthermore he treats them as real, in that they are aspects and objects of belief appearing to the mind as concrete images though they are not objectively existent. Or if they are, then it is not for the reasons of demonic influence usually given by the believer. Such an attitude of stressing the psychological reality together with the acknowledgment that belief may have its physical exemplifications would be particularly attractive to Graves. For some years he experienced the physical and psychological ramifications of a repugnant supranatural reality. To him, Frazer's savages and ancient civilizations were not simple-mindedly confusing the nature of reality, they were responding to it.

On occasion Graves moves his dramatic situations from the past, in which such beliefs were literally held, to the present, where their invocation functions as metaphor. He does so in the hopes of gaining a terminology and arrangement of scene that will permit him to render states of mind and feeling otherwise inaccessible to the modern temperament. Such is the case with "Ancestors" in which the narrator is visited on New Year's Eve by the spirits of the dead, who are summoned or attracted by the aroma of the narrator's mulled port. At first this appears to be an established festival in miniature, a survival of the custom of ritual libations offered to the dead in the hopes of placating them and enjoining their good offices. It turns in the course of the poem into an exposé and renunciation of the dead and the past. The spirits, who appear quickly, lose their awesome appearance as they reveal themselves to be little more than deceased topers cadging drinks and so to "have small pride or breeding left." So debased are they that they wish the same fate for the narrator as they suffered themselves:

> "May this young man in drink grown wise
> Die, as we also died, in drink!"

To this he responds immediately and vigorously:

> Their reedy voices I abhor,
> I am alive at least, and young,
> I dash their swill upon the floor:
> Let them lap grovelling, tongue to tongue.

The anthropological notion of the spirits of the dead and the apotropaic ritual due them allow Graves to bring into conjunction a complex of feelings that can be responded to sequentially. This complex includes such ideas as respect for ancestors and tradition, the continuity of civilized present and pagan, barbarous past (seen in the perpetuation of the festal rite), contempt for the obsessed who abandon all notions of dignity and become animal-like in the eagerness of their greed, and the self-righteous pride in life of the young. What the poem does is permit us to witness an interior drama. In its scenes one individual realizes through intimate contact with the past the insufficiency of it when superstitiously venerated. Hence, he rejects it in favor of self-sufficiency, which in its own way is shown to be of nearly equal inadequacy as a basis for living. In short, the poem is a double revelation of the falseness of past and present, old and young, dead and living. As the Circean imagery of the final stanza, quoted above, tells us, to transform men from the foolish animality of cockerels to the disgusting bestiality of swine is to work a magic whose blackness inescapably corrupts the wizard.

In the main, these attempts to present spirits and magic directly in contemporary life and scenes are not terribly successful. They resemble in effect some of Lawrence's short stories which treat ghosts literally and seriously. Much more successful are those poems in which Graves locates spells and demons in the world of dreams and nightmares. Here his study of Freud, Rivers, and the rest merges fruitfully with his exploration of anthropological treatments of magic and superstition like *The Golden Bough*. They combine to stress the reality of the dream experience as well as its links with the materials and functions of myth. Thus, though the nightmare usually predominates in the poems, on occasion Graves will treat dream as having some of the enchantment and literary delight of the myth narrative. Thus in "What Did I Dream?" the interrupted pleasant, humorous dream is sought again in sleep because it is "The finest entertainment known, / And given rag-cheap."

More characteristic of the awesome psychic tremors invoked by dreams is the experience in "Down." There the dreamer feels that he has inadvertently "magicked space" so that he is able to pass ghostlike through the most solid of objects. Yet the dream is not one exhibiting him as in control of his movements. Rather, in the powerful closing lines he is shown to be a helpless victim:

> Falling, falling! Day closed up behind him.
> Now stunned by the violent subterrene flow
> Of rivers, whirling down to hiss below
> On the flame-axis of this terrible earth;
> Toppling upon their waterfall, O spirit . . .

This shows a close resemblance in imagery to "Instructions to the Orphic Adept" and to Jane Harrison's account of the visionary rites at Trophonius. Hence appalling though this vision is, the lines suggest that this experience too is a ritual trial and confrontation leading to a clearer understanding of ordinary existence, which in itself appears as a kind of exaltation of life.

The marginal character of dreams, their role as rites of transition that distinguish two worlds is not always as vivid or threatening as in "Down." Thus "Through Nightmare" does not stress the terror but the admiration felt by the lover for his beloved who recounts the adventure. What is admired, though, is precisely her courage in enduring the mysterious journey of dream:

> . . . that you should travel
> Through nightmare to a lost and moated land,
> Who are timorous by nature.

Like Frazer's primitive tribes, Graves presents the dream experience as a journey, one in which the soul wanders far from its normal resting place, the body. At the same time, he also hints at the connection of dream and myth. Thus he points out that the inhabitants of a dream, the dramatis personae so to speak, "carry / Time looped so river-wise about their house / There's no way in by history's road / To name or number them." The dream is impregnable to the linear progressions of public history with its dates, battles, laws, and famous persons. It may, however, yield, out of sympathy and likeness, to myth with its cyclical patterns, indifference to probability, space, and time, and sensitivity to the psychic pressures of its maker. Perhaps because of this implied relationship between dream and myth the beloved is enjoined to "Never be disenchanted of / That place you sometimes dream yourself into," an injunction suggesting untold benefits lie in that distant realm.

What these treasures may be is implied most clearly by "In Procession" and "The Land of Whipperginny," which between them render the personal and intrapersonal dimensions of the goal. In the former, the narrator contrasts the dream and waking worlds as the materials of vision and expression. Then he identifies the latter with "the town of Hell" whose features he recounts in barren and cowardly fashion. By contrast the dream world is a "sudden moment" of vision in which he sees

> Carnival wagons
> With their saints and their dragons

On the scroll of my teeming mind:
The Creation and Flood
With our Saviour's Blood
And fat Silenus' flagons,
And every rare beast
From the South and East,
Both greatest and least,
On and on,
In endless, variant procession.

Out of this is born his desire to convey to the world all the
"Glories of land and sea, / Of Heaven glittering free" so that
it might feel the wonder of the paradisiacal scenes he himself
sees. These scenes are essentially a child's version of folklore
tales of fulfilled desire, of attainment of an enchanted promised
land, variously called "the Delectable Land," "the Land of the
Crooked Stiles," "the Fortunate Isles," "the Land of the Gold
Man," and "the Land of Whipperginny." This folklore motif
now dwindled to a nursery tale derives from or is inspired by a
vision whose images suggest a medieval religious pageant while
also carrying an undercurrent of the original Mediterranean
complex of dying gods and vegetative fertility rituals. From this
it is clear that Graves here is dramatizing the parallel courses of
dream and myth. He is also enunciating Frazer's view that many
of our central beliefs and desires today derive in an unbroken
continuity from ancient and primitive customs of which the dying
god is one of the most preeminent.

In this way he also renders Frazer's point about the mis-
understanding and dwindling of importance of rituals and
myths. As they become detached from one another, so their
meaning is lost or debased. Because the narrator does not
recognize the original mythic and ritualistic nature of, say, the
Land of Whipperginny he is incapable of celebrating it in tales.
Instead he must yield to the more pressing reality of the modern,
urbanized "Town of Hell— / A huddle of dirty woes / And
houses in fading rows / Straggled through space." If he realized
the mythic ground of the Delectable Land, he would not be

shamed out of his desire for it by the tawdry, gloomy sight of a cross between a Lawrence mining town and an English Midland manufacturing city. He would understand that the images of creation, sacrifice, and saturnalian abandon bespeak a more fundamental reality than that of any industrial inferno. As their capitalized abstractions suggest, they represent the perennial archetypes in terms of which human existence is structured. They are not the adventitious concretions of a specific, and therefore limited, historical moment. This realization, however, is as far beyond the narrator-dreamer as its mythic intimations are faint. Thus he is subjected to the tyranny of the actual in the light of which his central achievement is to define his life negatively as "This Town of Hell / Where between sleep and sleep I dwell." And even this he does unwittingly or at least without a full awareness of the meaning and reality of his *definiens*.

The isolated individual is vouchsafed a vision of the treasures found in dream and myth, but he is not able to communicate what he has seen. When two people, lovers, confront the trials and terrors of the world of fantasy, imagination, whether in dream or not, they can surmount the threatening or foreboding appearance of the natural world. Their love is its own kind of communication and in the face of its message they are undisturbed by whether it is "Heaven, or Hell, or the Land of Whipperginny / That holds this fairy lustre, not yet understood." The scene—sunset in the woods where the sound of swaying trees is "Lugubriously twisted to a howling of whores"—carries an eerie fearfulness. But the lovers pass through it with equanimity since they can look forward to the assistance of "the risen Moon," the goddess of love and dreams. The foreboding of the second stanza cannot overthrow the serene confidence of their love. This is because the love is supported by the divine Moon who shortly will draw "us in secret by an ivory gate / To the fruit-plats and fountains of her silver city / Where lovers need not argue the tokens of fate." The way, in short, to fend off the horrors of demon and nightmare is to follow the ritual of the White Goddess, the moon. This means to fall in love and then to enter "her silver city," which is the architectural form of romantic beauty and pleasure and the antithesis of "the Town of Hell."

Pleasurable and fulfilling though this Endymion-like lunar universe may be, we cannot forget that the moon-goddess is described as regarding the lovers "with pity." This emotion may be directed at their originally being isolated in an ominous landscape. Yet in view of the total perspective afforded by Graves's work on the moon-goddess, it is more likely directed at the future grief and disappointment inevitably to be experienced by the lovers. The cyclical movement of the White Goddess from fruition to death, from love to disenchantment, obtains in the world of dreams as well as in the waking universe. Such is the theme of "The Window Sill." It presents the demise of love and its discovery through the medium of a dream which portends a similar discovery in the waking world. Like *The Golden Bough*, the poem presents the belief that "Presage and caveat not only seem / To come in dream, / But do so come in dream." Just as Frazer's primitives see their dreams as true, so does Graves's narrator. He finds, despite her protestations of continued love, his beloved's betrayal of him embodied in the nightmarish disclosure of "Each breast a rose, / A white and cankered rose." The Blakean overtones merge with the goddess's vgetative nature as set forth in such poems as "The Song of Blodeuwedd" to tell us in unmistakable fashion that Julia the beloved is also the White Goddess in her aspect of betrayer of her lover.

Even more sharply detailed horror experienced through dream is found in "The Succubus." It is the antithesis of "The Land of Whipperginny" insofar as it sees the dream consummation of love as nauseous rather than idyllic. Instead of the "longed-for beauty" with "halo'd breast, firm belly and long, slender thigh," the fantasy-lover finds himself overwhelmed by "a devil-woman" who lustfully surges toward him "with hot face, / With paunched and uddered carcase." Horrifying though the scene and experience may be, the purpose is not to show simply that the demonic world is capable of sexual attacks as well as psychological forays. Instead, the poet takes a resolutely moral tack. The succubus is the dream concomitant of the man's desires and the appropriate reward and response to them. Her sexual assault interrogates the morality of his fantasies of passion: "is the fancy grosser than your lusts were gross?" And back of this indictment of the debasing of love is a charge more mythic than moral. The succubus is the goddess's revenge on anyone who attempts to demean her and her rites, for she is not to be summoned casually for pleasurable dalliance. Neither will she submit to those who either through despair, fear, or laziness seek to provide themselves with a fantasy substitute for her real presence. Thus, the man who pursues love only in his mind, in dream and fantasy, does not truly honor the goddess. Therefore he must suffer the fate he has sought to avoid by indulgence in fantasy gratification: pain, frustration, and disappointment.

From the foregoing it is clear that the world of demon and dream impinges on the human world as threat, as trial or test, and as punishment. They do so largely through a concreteness of temporality, either as presence or portent. The net effect of the various modes in which dreams operate is the establishment of their reality, a reality that is on the same ontological plane as that of the physical universe. The world of dreams and demons is not a mere aberrant intrusion of unreality into the real. It is a form of reality subsisting in its own right and capable of either friendly or hostile relations with the waking consciousness and its environment. As a result, it is imperative to grasp the laws by which it operates and the relations obtaining between the two worlds. In this way one may live and work and love effectively and satisfyingly in each.

The clearest statement of this existential imperative occurs in the poem "Alice," which, unsurprisingly enough, deals with Lewis Carroll's great creation, described by Graves as "that prime heroine of our nation." According to the poem, not only has Alice anticipated the possibility of a looking-glass world, she has also mastered its rules and laws of movement and advance.

More important, however, than her demonstration of adaptability and cultural relativity is her unrestrained credence of the actuality of the world of dream, fantasy, and myth:

> But her greater feat
> Was rounding these adventures off complete:
> Accepting them, when safe returned again,
> As queer but true—not only in the main
> True, but as true as anything you'd swear to,
> The usual three dimensions you are heir to.

She regards her adventure world as real because she is able to grasp the discontinuity existing between it and the so-called ordinary world:

> For Alice though a child could understand
> That neither did this chance-discovered land
> Make nohow or contrariwise the clean
> Dull round of mid-Victorian routine,
> Nor did Victoria's golden rule extend
> Beyond the glass: it came to the dead end
> Where empty hearses turn about; thereafter
> Begins that lubberland of dream and laughter,
> The red-and-white-flower-spangled hedge, the grass
> Where Apuleius pastured his Gold Ass,
> Where young Gargantua made whole holiday . . .

By accepting the clear evidence of her senses consistently, Alice is able to recognize the obvious—that consistency is not necessarily reality. She sees that contradictory experiences are merely different experiences so long as they do not share the same laws of probability and natural order. The human world is irremediably dualistic, but this is not an insurmountable barrier to relations between the two halves. All that is required is the understanding that items in the two spheres are related through their sharing analogous functions; that is, they are related by

homology rather than identity. So seen, one can regard the whole
of dreams and demons as, like those of nature and man, a place
of enchantment and enslavement, fear and hope, friend and
enemy, love and death. Thus, like all of man's antagonists, whom
in a sense it symbolizes, this world is never finally and irrevocably
overcome or defeated. Like the Blatant Beast of "Saint," it
survives all human rites of expulsion and clings steadfastly to
man of whom it is an integral part and projection. It can, however, be held at bay through the judicious employment of
language. This allows man to "Retreat from too much joy or too
much fear" while at the same time maintaining contact with
immediate experience, with "the rose, the dark sky and the
drums" whose unmediated presence can inspire madness. In
short, man can best live in the world of nature, persons, and
demons by becoming a poet, a disciplined, dedicated user of
language.

## II

This view of the poet is implicit in "The Cool Web." He is
the person who preserves a dialectical tension between the use of
language as a deflector of the shock of raw experience and as a
retreat from reality. The polarity of being able in magical fashion
to "spell away the overhanging night . . . the soldiers and the
fright" and of being engulfed by the sea of words where the
only fate is to "coldly die / In brininess and volubility" has
important implications for the modes of poetry in which Graves
has chosen to work. Most obviously Graves is a lyric poet;
virtually all of his love poems—those that deal at least by
implication with fertility or phallic myths, deities, and rituals—
are in this form. At the same time, those poems that deal with the
White Goddess and her consort, their roles and rituals, extend
beyond the lyric mode. They endeavor to make some larger, more
inclusive statement about man, his place in the world and
society, and the particular character of his cultural history. In
short, taken as a whole, these poems may fairly be said to have
epic aspirations, and in this respect bear comparison with those

poems of Yeats inspired by *A Vision*. Both Graves and Yeats have written fragments of an epic whose outlines are sketched in workbooks entitled *The White Goddess* and *A Vision* respectively. Lyric and epic, even the putative epic, can be construed as employing language to control experience, to shape through distancing its raw, jagged angularity into bearable and meaningful verbal forms. But if Graves is to achieve the dialectical tension he envisages in the workings of language, he must set over against the lyric and epic poems a mode whose function is to move toward a controlled release of language so that experience and reality are apprehended more nearly with a felt sense of their awful power. This he does in those poems that carry a satiric inflection, many of which are elaborations of classical legends.

In singling out Graves's satires rooted in classical legend, there is no claim that all his treatments of such classical material is satiric in manner. What these poems offer is a convenient and illuminating perspective from which to draw together the overriding pattern of Graves's poetic work. The legendary material draws us in the direction of the epic mode and tone, of solemn regard for the profundities of tradition. At the same time, the satiric attitude pulls against the ritualizing pattern that turns people into heroes and gods. As one might anticipate, since Graves devotes more poems to the theme of love than to any other, his satires reflect this trend, too. In poems like "Ulysses," "Galatea and Pygmalion," "Theseus and Ariadne," and "Penthesileia," we move in a variety of ways behind the traditional story or surface of the legend. By so doing, we see either what its protagonists' real natures were or how the legend makes its own ironic commentary on the rationales and motives of human feelings.

All of the above-mentioned poems reveal aspects of sexual love or what has hitherto been called the phallic ritual that the rites of devotion demanded by the lyric mask. "Ulysses," for instance, presents the wanderer's dilemma as basically sexual:

To the much-tossed Ulysses, never done

With woman whether gowned as wife or whore,
Penelope and Circe seemed as one:
She like a whore made his lewd fancies run,
And wifely she a hero to him bore.

All his other adventures are simply forms or variations on this
sexual puzzle of whether one can validly discriminate between
the major relations in which woman stands to man sexually. The
lightninglike transformations from wife to whore and back again
and his own confusion as to which is which produce the obstacles
that keep him a wayfarer for twenty years. The pleasures and
terrors of the flesh are, the poem goes on, the physiological
ground of both the confusion and duality of woman's role. And
yet it is through sexuality itself that Ulysses, the paradigmatic
man, discovers the hard truth of his passionate dialectic, which
if it does not solve the problem yet permits him to endure it:

Triumph of flesh and afterwards to find
Still those same terrors wherewith flesh was wracked.

Here the dutiful ritual of obedience to the love goddess is seen
from the inside. To the eye of satire the ritual therefore appears
less like a free ceremony of homage than a confining, circum-
scribing prison out of which man can scarcely hope ever to
break. Since "He loathed the fraud, yet would not bed alone,"
Ulysses as the sexual man emerges as a comic figure aware that
his difficulties are self-created. Nevertheless, he persists in them
out of some fundamental trait of character. As a result, in the
end his devotion to the idea of Ithaca and all it stands for is
seen to be founded on the fact that "All lands to him were
Ithaca." Behind the devoted husband of myth stands the
relentless promiscuity of a man separated from his woman that
reality dictates. Yet Graves's intent is not to drive a wedge
between these two and so to diminish both. Instead, myth and
reality are merged so that the puritanic idealism of the husband
and the callous self-indulgence of the lover are both purged.
Satire here operates not so much for excoriation or moral correc-

tion as for illumination of human motives, which exist in a kind
of limbo between *is* and *ought.*

If "Ulysses" reveals the comic dilemma posed by the phallic
ritual, both "Galatea and Pygmalion" and "Theseus and
Ariadne" exhibit the irony of making complacent assumptions
about its course. In so doing, they satirically rebuke male
arrogance. They simultaneously effect an implicit defense of the
woman as goddess and a sympathetic revenge for the suffering
she humanly endures at the hands of man. Pygmalion, in
Graves's poem, makes his statue-woman not out of disgust for
the immortality and wantonness of his neighbors, as some
accounts have it, but "by greed enchanted." Since she responds
lubriciously "With low responses to his drunken raptures," his
greed is clearly sexually focused. Pygmalion's action and fate is
substantially that of the character in "The Succubus." He makes
a sexual object that will afford him complete fulfillment, but as a
result finds himself with the opposite of what he had anticipated.
Instead of fulfillment he finds frustration. Instead of his own
fame it is her nature that is celebrated, for he has made a stone-
woman better than he thought:

> . . . schools of eager connoisseurs beset
> Her single person with perennial suit;
> Whom she (a judgment on the jealous artist)
> Admitted rankly to a comprehension
> Of themes that crowned her own, not his repute.

Having constructed an object of phallic beauty and pleasure, he
finds that others are prepared to worship and celebrate it in the
only way appropriate. The sexual vitality of Galatea, Graves's
*Greek Myths* suggests, is the incarnation of Aphrodite. This
quality is a testimony to the vitality of her life and its independence of any maker as well as to the fate of any who
presumes to violate the nature of woman by ignoring the goddess
resident in her. Unlike the poems in the epic mode, however, the
satires expose such creatures of *hybris* not to death but to
mockery and laughter. To be a cuckold, not a corpse, is the fate

Gravesian satire holds out to the unwary and the disrespectful.

"Theseus and Ariadne" has a similar pattern though in its case the fate of the man is to remain ignorant of his own self-deception. The poem deals with the separate reactions of the legendary lovers some time after his desertion of her. Theseus is presented first as thinking of her with an indulgent sentimentality of guilt that scarcely touches his deeper feelings. He recognizes that " 'Deep sunk in my erroneous past / She haunts the ruins and the ravaged lawns.' " But he does so amid "dreams" and "sighs." These suggest that he is less impelled by contrition than by satisfaction with his own power to command her disappointed, grieving love. Yet when the scene turns to Ariadne, the folly of Theseus's self-image as creator of love-lorn maidens is evident:

> Of him, now all is done, she never dreams
> But calls a living blessing down upon
> What he supposes rubble and rank grass;
> Playing the queen to nobler company.

His mistake is to think that he has left her bereft of her role as woman. Actually she is realizing in and through nature itself her ultimate role, that of the ruler of the living.

Perhaps the furthest extent to which the satiric defense of the phallic ritual is carried takes place in "Penthesileia." It deals with one of those classical legends that suddenly reveals the primitive passion and savage beliefs concealed beneath images of serene, timeless beauty and philosophical acceptance that are usually thought to make up the classical attitude. Graves follows closely the story of the Amazonian queen who fought on the Trojan side until killed by Achilles, who then fell in love with her body, committed necrophilia on it, and slew Thersites when accused of unnatural lust. The first two stanzas, which recount the legend, move in a jaunty vigor that treats the perversion with a kind of frontline candor and offhandedness which make it nearly comic in effect. As the last stanza makes clear, the poem is actually engaged in a corrective realignment of the prevailing sexual ethic.

The mythic illustration provides both shock and distance, subject and perspective. In these terms the limitless scope of the truly apprehended phallic ritual is clearly indicated:

> Yet Penthesileia, hailed by Prince Achilles
> On the Elysian plain, pauses to thank him
> For avenging her insulted womanhood
> With sacrifice.

The vengeance exacted by Achilles is, in reality, twofold. First, there is the slaying of Thersites because by his "obscene snigger" he sought to demean the significance of the phallic ritual enacted by Achilles with the Amazon; that is, he saw in it no more than necrophilia, the fruitless perversion of the ultimate act of life into a dead sexual object. Second, the sacrifice to her insulted womanhood is not only the dead body of Thersites but the necrophiliac act itself, the merging of the living body of Achilles with that of the dead woman. The ultimate insult would be to contemplate her naked corpse sheerly as a physical object rather than as one of desire. Thus, Achilles restores to her her role as a woman. In so doing, he shows that the limitation of the phallic ritual to normal or moral acts is to emasculate it as the celebration of life perennial. What this satire does in effect is to present the ritual of the White Goddess in the most horrifying fashion conceivable and then to show that the horror is the product of the ignorance and straitened imaginations of society. After the public enactment of the ritual, "Some gasped, some groaned, some bawled their indignation." By this they divulge that they have capitulated to the thinghood, the objectivity of death, for they have ceased to see in "that fierce white naked corpse" the figure of the eternal immortal White Goddess who is the emblem of life unquenchable for man and his world.

While Graves has written a number of other satires and grotesques, those examined suffice to define the role of the genre in his canon. As has been indicated, satire is the medium by which the mythic life principle is protected and revenged.

Originating in curse and magic, satire is the poet's weapon for preserving the existence he values. It is the only form in which man can survive his antagonists and celebrate the beauty, terror, and exaltation that rule his life. It is in this light that we should consider Graves's satires, not only those utilizing classical legend but also those that attack the stultifying absurdities of orthodoxies of all sorts, whether religious, social, scientific, historical, or mythical. In every case, the ultimate aim of the satire is to prevent that dissolution of awe and mystery which inevitably follows from the rigid dogmatism of any abstract theory no matter how simplified in form. Upon awe and mystery depend, according to Graves, not merely the worship of the White Goddess but that deep-seated apprehension of the nature of human life for which she stands. Like Frazer, Graves has an acute sense both of the pattern and the puzzle in man's world of speech and action, myth and ritual, theory and practice, and it is to the preservation of both that his career has been dedicated.

# Index